THE STATES AND THE NATION SERIES, of which this volume is a part, is designed to assist the American people in a serious look at the ideals they have espoused and the experiences they have undergone in the history of the nation. The content of every volume represents the scholarship, experience, and opinions of its author. The costs of writing and editing were met mainly by grants from the National Endowment for the Humanities, a federal agency. The project was administered by the American Association for State and Local History, a nonprofit learned society, working with an Editorial Board of distinguished editors, authors, and historians, whose names are listed below.

Maine

A Bicentennial History

Charles E. Clark

W. W. Norton & Company, Inc.
New York

American Association for State and Local History
Nashville

Library of Congress Cataloguing-in-Publication Data

Clark, Charles E   1929–
  Maine.

  (The States and the Nations series)
  Bibliography: p.
  Includes index.
  1. Maine—History. I. Title. II. Series.
F19.C54   974.1   77-22864
ISBN 0–393–05653–8

Published and distributed by
W. W. Norton & Company, Inc.
500 Fifth Avenue
New York, New York 10036

Printed in the United States of America

1 2 3 4 5 6 7 8 9 0

To
Clarence and Beatrice Clark
who kindly arranged for me to be a native
and
who will stand forever in the center
of my own image of Maine

Contents

Illustrations

ACKNOWLEDGMENTS

Pulling together, sorting out, thinking about meanings, writing doggedly—these tasks, not new research, are the main jobs in making a brief historical essay. The essayist draws on his previous research, his observations and reflections, the people he knows, and the books and articles he reads. He must rely especially on the last for most of the actual facts of history outside the areas of his own research.

In putting together this essay on the history of Maine and its meaning to me, therefore, I have had to draw heavily on the work of several specialists in Maine history. It is fitting that I acknowledge my great debt to them now.

Chief among them are three historians at the University of Maine at Orono, where a large share of the contemporary research in the history of Maine is going on. They are Ronald F. Banks, a specialist in the early national period and author of the pre-eminent work on the movement for Maine statehood; David C. Smith, our principal specialist in the history of the lumbering and papermaking industries of Maine; and Clarence A. Day, who practically invented the field of Maine agricultural history and then became its chief practitioner before his retirement several years ago. I have also relied heavily in several parts of the essay upon William Hutchinson Rowe's standard *Maritime History of Maine* and Edward Chase Kirkland's remarkable two-volume study, *Men, Cities, and Transportation: A Study in New England History, 1820–1900*.

In a bibliographical guide published by the Maine Historical Society in 1974, I commented harshly and a bit flippantly upon Louis C. Hatch's five-volume *Maine: A History* as a contribution to the history of colonial Maine. I see no reason to alter that judgment with respect to the colonial era, but do want to round out the record by acknowledging the many times during my voyage through the unfamiliar waters of the nineteenth century that I have referred with rewarding results to that very book, the bulk of which has since been reprinted in a single volume by the New Hampshire Publishing Company. Hatch's work also proved valuable to me for its inclusion of a fine essay on the Indians of Maine written by Fannie Hardy Eckstorm, a Maine institution. That essay provided me with the starting point of this book, and some of Mrs. Eckstorm's other extensive historical-anthropological writings helped begin my education in an area I should like to know better.

In addition to noting that several specialists in Maine history and their graduate students are at work at the University of Maine at Orono, where the *University of Maine Studies* occasionally carries the results of their research, I think it important to draw attention to the work of the Maine Academic Historians, an association of professional historians from institutions throughout the state. Through meetings, publications, and mutual encouragement, and with the support of the Maine Historical Society, this group has served as an important stimulus to the study and teaching of Maine history since its founding in 1972 under the leadership of John W. Hakola of the University of Maine at Orono, James S. Leamon of Bates College, and Joel W. Eastman of the University of Maine at Portland-Gorham. *The Maine Historical Society Quarterly,* in addition to serving in the usual ways as the organ of a state historical society, has served as a principal outlet for the work of this group. I have made heavy use of this journal, and of the Maine Historical Society's valuable Bibliographical Guide Series, in compiling the materials for this essay.

In addition to the "facts" and their interpretation, this essay contains some generalizations and judgments that are neither proven nor provable. Readers of a certain cast of mind will object to that. I understand why, but can do nothing to satisfy their objections, for to be satisfied they would have to have known pretty much the same Maine people I have known. I have felt obliged to describe Maine as I see it, and when that duty has necessitated going beyond the documentable into my own subjective impressions of growing up and spending many adult years in a variety of northern New England settings, I have done so.

Several individuals have been especially kind and helpful during the year in which this historical essay was being written. Gerald E. Morris, the genial director of the Maine Historical Society and editor of its publications, has extended to me greater courtesies than I had a right to expect. Thomas L. Gaffney, the society's curator of manuscripts, helped with some hints and suggestions. My brother, Llewellyn E. Clark, supplied some useful anecdotes and occasional insights regarding a part of Maine that is outside my ordinary experience. Robert M. Mennel, chairman, and my other colleagues in the department of history at the University of New Hampshire, have supported if not indulged me, and Timothy C. Jacobson of the AASLH has encouraged and forgiven me. Linda Stimson cheerfully did the typing. Two of my closest friends at the University of New Hampshire, Hans Heilbronner and Donald M. Murray, have done me the kindness of reading and responding to the manuscript. For Don Murray, in fact, this has come to be an old story; he has lived with this and my other work so long and so well that I don't understand why he is not tired of it. But I am grateful. The same goes, many times over, for my wife Margery.

C.E.C.

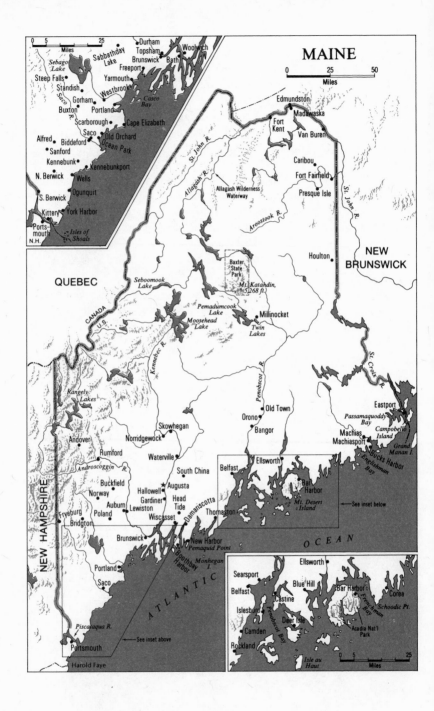

MAINE

0   25   50
Miles

0 5   25
Miles

Durham
Topsham
Woolwich
Sabbathday
Lake
Brunswick   Bath
Sebago
Lake   Freeport
Steep Falls   Yarmouth
Standish   Westbrook
Gorham   Casco
Buxton   Bay
Portland
Scarborough   Cape Elizabeth
Saco   Old Orchard
Alfred   Ocean Park
Sanford   Biddeford
Kennebunk
N. Berwick   Kennebunkport
Wells
S. Berwick   Ogunquit
Kittery   York Harbor
Ports-
mouth   Isles of
N.H.   Shoals

Edmundston
Madawaska
Fort
Kent   Van Buren
St. John R.
Caribou
Fort Fairfield
Presque Isle

Allagash Wilderness
Waterway

Aroostook R.

Houlton

NEW
BRUNSWICK

QUEBEC

Seboomook
Lake

Baxter
State
Park

Mt. Katahdin,
5,268 ft.

Pemadumcook
Lake   Millinocket

Moosehead
Lake   Twin
Lakes

CANADA
U.S.

Kennebec R.

Rangely
Lakes

Penobscot R.

St. Croix R.

Eastport

Old Town
Orono   Passamaquoddy
Bay   Campobello
Island
Bangor   Machias
Machiasport   Grand
Manan I.
Bucks Harbor
Englishman
Bay

Skowhegan

Norridgewock

Andover

Rumford

Waterville

Androscoggin R.

Buckfield

Norway

South China

Belfast   Ellsworth

See inset below

Bar
Harbor

Mt. Desert
Island

Hallowell   Augusta
Gardiner   Head
Auburn   Lewiston   Tide
Poland   Wiscasset
Damariscotta
Thomaston

Fryeburg
Bridgton

Brunswick

New Harbor
Pemaquid Point
Boothbay   Monhegan
Harbor   I.

OCEAN

NEW HAMPSHIRE

Portland

Saco

Piscataqua R.

ATLANTIC

See inset above

Portsmouth

Harold Faye

Ellsworth

Searsport
Blue Hill
Belfast
Castine   Bar Harbor
Islesboro   Corea
Schoodic Pt.
Freshman
Bay

Deer Isle   Acadia Nat'l
Park
Camden
Penobscot Bay

Rockland

Isle au
Haut   0 5   25
Miles

Invitation to the Reader

IN 1807, former President John Adams argued that a complete history of the American Revolution could not be written until the history of change in each state was known, because the principles of the Revolution were as various as the states that went through it. Two hundred years after the Declaration of Independence, the American nation has spread over a continent and beyond. The states have grown in number from thirteen to fifty. And democratic principles have been interpreted differently in every one of them.

We therefore invite you to consider that the history of your state may have more to do with the bicentennial review of the American Revolution than does the story of Bunker Hill or Valley Forge. The Revolution has continued as Americans extended liberty and democracy over a vast territory. John Adams was right: the states are part of that story, and the story is incomplete without an account of their diversity.

The Declaration of Independence stressed life, liberty, and the pursuit of happiness; accordingly, it shattered the notion of holding new territories in the subordinate status of colonies. The Northwest Ordinance of 1787 set forth a procedure for new states to enter the Union on an equal footing with the old. The Federal Constitution shortly confirmed this novel means of building a nation out of equal states. The step-by-step process through which territories have achieved self-government and national representation is among the most important of the Founding Fathers' legacies.

The method of state-making reconciled the ancient conflict between liberty and empire, resulting in what Thomas Jefferson called an empire for liberty. The system has worked and remains unaltered, despite enormous changes that have taken

xiii

place in the nation. The country's extent and variety now sur-
pass anything the patriots of '76 could likely have imagined.
The United States has changed from an agrarian republic into a
highly industrial and urban democracy, from a fledgling nation
into a major world power. As Oliver Wendell Holmes remarked
in 1920, the creators of the nation could not have seen completely how it and its constitution and its states would develop.
Any meaningful review in the bicentennial era must consider
what the country has become, as well as what it was.

The new nation of equal states took as its motto *E Pluribus
Unum*—"out of many, one." But just as many peoples have
become Americans without complete loss of ethnic and cultural
identities, so have the states retained differences of character.
Some have been superficial, expressed in stereotyped images—
big, boastful Texas, "sophisticated" New York, "hillbilly"
Arkansas. Other differences have been more real, sometimes instructively, sometimes amusingly; democracy has embraced
Huey Long's Louisiana, bilingual New Mexico, unicameral Ne-
braska, and a Texas that once taxed fortunetellers and spawned
politicians called "Woodpecker Republicans" and "Skunk
Democrats." Some differences have been profound, as when
South Carolina secessionists led other states out of the Union in
opposition to abolitionists in Massachusetts and Ohio. The result was a bitter Civil War.

The Revolution's first shots may have sounded in Lexington
and Concord; but fights over what democracy should mean and
who should have independence have erupted from Pennsylvania's Gettysburg to the "Bleeding Kansas" of John Brown,
from the Alamo in Texas to the Indian battles at Montana's
Little Bighorn. Utah Mormons have known the strain of isolation; Hawaiians at Pearl Harbor, the terror of attack; Georgians
during Sherman's march, the sadness of defeat and devastation.
Each state's experience differs instructively; each adds understanding to the whole.

The purpose of this series of books is to make that kind of understanding accessible, in a way that will last in value far
beyond the bicentennial fireworks. The series offers a volume
on every state, plus the District of Columbia—fifty-one, in all.

Each book contains, besides the text, a view of the state through eyes other than the author's—a "photographer's essay," in which a skilled photographer presents his own personal perceptions of the state's contemporary flavor.

We have asked authors not for comprehensive chronicles, nor for research monographs or new data for scholars. Bibliographies and footnotes are minimal. We have asked each author for a summing up—interpretive, sensitive, thoughtful, individual, even personal—of what seems significant about his or her state's history. What distinguishes it? What has mattered about it, to its own people and to the rest of the nation? What has it come to now?

To interpret the states in all their variety, we have sought a variety of backgrounds in authors themselves and have encouraged variety in the approaches they take. They have in common only these things: historical knowledge, writing skill, and strong personal feelings about a particular state. Each has wide latitude for the use of the short space. And if each succeeds, it will be by offering you, in your capacity as a *citizen* of a state *and* of a nation, stimulating insights to test against your own.

James Morton Smith
General Editor

Maine

1

Images

*T*HEY came east. Untold generations of migration from beginnings as yet unidentified by science led one branch of the great Algonquin family to the wooded shores of the far northeast. They broke through the dark forests of pine, spruce, and hemlock into the light of day, and saw the heaving North Atlantic assault the ledges and boulders at the edge of the continent with elemental force and then retreat and then attack again. Today, hundreds of long-buried shell heaps mark the summer encampments near the shore where they came year after year to dig soft-shelled clams and shiny quahogs from the tidal mudflats. Here also, where the aboriginal Red Paint people had lived and vanished centuries before, Algonquins picked clusters of oysters from their half-exposed beds and gathered fallen acorns from around nearby oak trees. Gradually, during more uncounted generations after the breakthrough, they dispersed themselves in definite groupings along the coast, each tribe settling at a location whose description became its name. The sorting out was still in process when the white man came.

For those who drifted northeastward along the shore from Massachusetts Bay to become the Penacooks, the Sacos, the Androscoggins, the Kennebecs, the Wawenocks, the Penobscots, the Passamaquoddies, and their various subtribes, there was a special name that applied to them all. It was "Wabanaki," which meant "living at the sunrise," or, to use the felici-

tous term of a nineteenth-century scholar, "Dawnlander." [1]
And so the Abnaki (as the name is now usually rendered in English) spoke of his place with an image that captured his ancestral memory of eastward movement. He called it Dawnland—the East.

But from Europe, they came west. In 1497, when John Cabot touched Newfoundland or whatever it was, he thought—as Columbus had thought five years earlier and 2,000 miles to the southward—he was in the Orient. Subsequent discoveries made it plain that a continent blocked the westward water route from Europe to the spices of India. With their minds set on the riches of the Orient, the northern Europeans, leaving the wealth of the southern empires to the Spaniards and the Portuguese, first came in quest, not of the wonders of North America but of the Northwest Passage. North America was for them not an opportunity, but an obstacle.

Sir Humphrey Gilbert told his fellow Englishmen how to find the Northwest Passage, and he led the way. American independence stands exactly halfway between us and the publication in 1576 of his *Discourse of a Discoverie for a new Passage to Cataia.* In accordance with his theory, many of the northern voyages followed the route of the Norsemen across the converging meridians at the top of the ocean, touching Greenland, sometimes exploring Davis Strait and Baffin Bay when these waterways were not choked with floating ice, and then following the Labrador Current southward to Newfoundland and Labrador, and finally to Nova Scotia. Or they might strike a direct course for Newfoundland, where North America reaches closest to Europe, perhaps exploring northward from there for the promised channel west to India.

But North America, unhandy barrier though it was, suggested still another idea to Sir Humphrey. It was he who first con-

1. The translation is that of Joseph Nicolar, quoted by Fannie Hardy Eckstorm from his *Life and Traditions of the Red Men* (Bangor, Me.: C. H. Glass & Co., printers, 1893). See Eckstorm, "The Indians of Maine," which appears as Chapter 3 in Louis Clinton Hatch, *Maine: A History* (1919; facsimile reprint ed., Somersworth, N.H.: New Hampshire Publishing Co., 1974), pp. 43, 45, 45n.

vinced Queen Elizabeth that the new land offered a chance to solve what everyone thought was a serious population problem. Why not, he suggested, form colonies there of surplus Englishmen? With a commission from the queen to explore and colonize any unclaimed lands he found, Sir Humphrey sent out an expedition in 1580 under John Walker to scout the hazy place called "Norumbega" that Englishmen knew lay somewhere on the "back side" of Nova Scotia. Walker returned, probably from Penobscot Bay, with some animal hides, which brought a good price in France, and reported that Norumbega not only was rich in furs but even had a silver mine. He may have been fooled, like many Americans who lived centuries after him, by the quartz and mica of Mount Battie at Camden. Sir Humphrey aimed to plant a colony in Norumbega, and had storms and shortages not broken up his expedition of 1583, he might have done so. His ship finally turned back to England and went down with all hands.

That was the end of one man's dream, but not of the succession of different beckoning images of the place that the Abnakis called the Dawnland. There was, for one thing, the northern European idea of where it was—on the backside of Nova Scotia, across the Bay of Fundy from the parts of North America that were best known. Not at all the Dawnland, but a mysterious, half-mythic country all girded with rock, where in latitudes too far south to yield the Northwest Passage, the ocean finally dashed itself to pieces in the long shadows of the forest that loomed before the setting sun.

But for many Europeans of the sixteenth century, this was not just any dimly known western land. It was *Norumbega,* which name alone furnished an image almost as compelling as that of its contemporary Latin counterpart, El Dorado. The difference was that for the legendary wealth of Central and South America, there was some basis in fact. Norumbega existed in the imagination alone.

From time beyond remembering, Western man had longed to find a paradise on earth, a place of innocence and plenty where he might begin life afresh, free from the restraints of his own history. Out of such imaginings, he had invented the Elysian

Fields, Atlantis, and Eden. And when he discovered America, his dreams of an earthly paradise became renewed, and he went there trustingly in quest of gold and everlasting youth. A combination of this ancient dream, the reality of solid gold and jewels in Mexico and Peru, and exaggerated travelers' tales, must have led to the myth of Norumbega, a fabulous city littered with gold and silver and "pyllors of Cristoll," located somewhere between Nova Scotia and Florida. For much of the sixteenth century, mapmakers commonly located this fabled land, which never existed anywhere except in gullible European minds, on the Penobscot River.

In 1524, Giovanni da Verrazzano, in the first documented case of a European actually laying eyes on the land of the Abnakis, labeled a point that could be near Penobscot Bay "Oranbega." He and his brother Girolamo, who made a world map that incorporated these discoveries in 1529, were innocent collaborators in spawning the legend of Norumbega. They are responsible, nobody can deny, for getting that Algonquin name (which means "quiet place between two rapids") on the map. But it is hardly their fault that their French and English successors over the next seven or eight decades embroidered it with fantasy. It was Samuel de Champlain who effectively demolished the myth by carefully exploring and mapping the coast in 1604. Finally in 1612, Marc Lescarbot, whose fellow Frenchmen had taken the leading role in building the legend, laid it to rest with the sardonic observation, "If that beautiful city has ever existed in nature, I should like to hear who destroyed it; for there are only a few cabins here and there, made of poles and covered with branches of trees or with skins." [2]

Besides putting Norumbega on the map, the Verrazzano brothers created the first recorded image of the Abnakis. Not far to the east of "Oranbega" on Girolamo's map is another name, this one in the Verrazzanos' own Italian: *"terra onde di mala gente."* There was good reason for a title as unflattering as "land of bad people." Unlike most explorers of the sixteenth

2. Sigmund Diamond, "Norumbega: New England Xanadu," *The American Neptune* 11 (April 1951): 106.

century, Verrazzano sailed from south to north. Some of the warmest recollections in his report to the king of France concern the Wampanoags of Narragansett Bay. The next native Americans he encountered, farther along the coast in the land of the Abnakis, were a far different matter. They consented to trade only by lowering a basket to a boat from "some rocks where the breakers were most violent," and "when we had nothing more to exchange and left them, the men made all the signs of scorn and shame that any brute creature would make, such as exhibiting their bare behinds and laughing immoderately." [3]

Apparently, these eastern Indians had done business with Europeans before and had been cheated or worse. Rape, kidnaping, murder—none of these is beyond possibility, and any one of them would account, not only for the rude trading manners but also for the frightening though ineffective flight of arrows that greeted a French landing party that Verrazzano led ashore. What frustrates the historian is his almost certain knowledge that European fishermen or traders were on this coast before Verrazzano saw it in 1524, and his despair at ever finding out who they were and exactly how early they came. Nobody knows how many adventurous, greedy, or lost sailors may have landed here without ever having written a letter, filed a report, or even made an entry in a long-lost log book. In any case, Verrazzano's image of the "bad people," though its own influence never amounted to much, certainly was shared in the seventeenth and eighteenth centuries by hundreds of English pioneer settlers whose relations with the descendants of these scornful bottom-barers were tragic for both sides.

There were images, then, of the land and its people, and there were also perceptions of man's relationship to the land, and ideas about its use and its future.

To the Abnaki, the life of man was as much a part of nature

3. Lawrence C. Wroth, *The Voyages of Giovanni da Verrazzano* (New Haven: Yale University Press, 1970), pp. 140–141 and maps, plate 2. The translation is a composite of that of Susan Tarrow in the work just cited and that of Samuel Eliot Morison in *The European Discovery of America: The Northern Voyages* (New York: Oxford University Press, 1971), p. 309.

as the life of the deer, the moose, and the beaver. Gluskabe, the Abnaki's amusing and tricky culture-hero who had made himself out of the dust left over from the creation of the first man, had made marks on the local landscape that affected man and animal alike. He had, for example, killed a monster frog that had caused a world drought, and the waters thus released rushed down toward the sea, forming the Penobscot River. He had captured and then distributed game animals over the world, distributed the tobacco plant, made and then softened the wind, moderated the seasons, tamed the dog, reduced the ferocious giant squirrel to a harmless size, and punished early men and women for various sins by changing them into toads and repulsive sea creatures.[4]

To kill an animal was for the Abnaki to participate in a preordained process that governed all nature. Each tribe of animal—the bear, the moose, the deer, the mink—had its own special powers and characteristics, just as man had his own, and he who killed an animal owed it the marks of respect appropriate to its kind. The woods, lakes, and streams harbored supernatural creatures, neither animal nor human, some friendly to man and some hostile. According to their nature, they gave help and advice, prophesied, seduced, annoyed, tricked, abducted, killed, or, in the case of certain female spirits, unintentionally harmed the men and children whom they lured with their longing cries. A handsome, supernaturally endowed personification of Mount Katahdin lived inside that impressive mountain with his family. Occasionally, according to various tales, he would take a Penobscot girl for his bride.[5]

The Abnaki's religion, his superstitions, his folklore, the organization of his tribe and clan, and his means and rituals of survival all reflected his intimacy with his landscape and his

---

4. Tales of Gluskabe figure prominently in Frank G. Speck's "Wawenock Myth Texts from Maine," *Bureau of American Ethnology, Forty-third Annual Report, 1925–1926* (Washington, D.C., 1928), 169–197, and, by the same author, "Penobscot Tales and Religious Beliefs," *Journal of American Folklore* 48 (January–March 1935): 5–12, 38–53.

5. Speck, "Penobscot Tales and Religious Beliefs," pp. 12–17, 66–70, 75–78, 84–85.

partnership with the other living things in it. And his world as he saw it, at least until the Europeans came, for the most part was unchanging.

Not so the world of the Europeans in the Age of Discovery. Far from it. The nation-state, a new thing whose nature was still only half-understood, provided the means of organizing and applying political power and acquiring wealth. Cities grew and flourished around the revival of shipping and commerce, and there men could gather at wharves and marketplaces to learn of new discoveries and distant peoples. Trade and learning rose together, and people changed in means and class, and even religion changed. In the cities, one could see the changes happen. Newfound territories across the Atlantic offered alluring opportunities for wealth and happiness, and supplied the makings of vision upon vision.

Whereas the Abnaki's image of his land reflected his own close partnership with it, the European's image of the same place sprang from his own experience somewhere else, and often was rooted deeply in his own past. It was not necessary to see this land to have an image of it, and to have a vision for it. The legend of Norumbega is a case in point. Another such vision had equally little to do with the forests, the lakes, the rivers, and the seaside ledges and marshes that composed the real landscape. It had to do instead with the feudal past that the new states and the new commerce of Europe were just now making obsolete.

For a thousand years, the power, the wealth, and the prestige of the nobility and gentry of Europe had rested upon the land. Armies had been raised, rents paid, hereditary privileges and obligations passed from father to son, titles granted and inherited, and kings obeyed, all on the basis of a hierarchical system of lordships that in the end depended upon the holding of land. The slow shift to a system in which wealth and political power depended more upon trade than upon the land did not happen overnight. Neither did the parallel movement from a loyalty based upon feudal lordship to a loyalty based upon residence in a territorial state. Nor did the eventual replacement of the old by the new bring about the automatic rejection of old assumptions and old values. Men and woman do not always recognize historical changes of which they are in the midst, and the more fundamental the change, the more difficult it is to discern it and act upon it. And even if people are aware of the change, they may continue to act upon assumptions that seem valid and to pursue values that remain enduring if not eternal.

This was how many Europeans regarded the land, especially when it seemed to be running out. To possess it with titles from a king and to exercise dominion over it—to possess it in a way that the Abnakis, who merely lived from it, would not have understood—these were the ambitions of a few men of power and means when it became apparent that whatever might become of the supply of land in Europe, there was plenty in America.

And so there arose a vision of the land of the Abnakis that we may call, with some license, "feudal."

Pierre du Guast, the Sieur de Monts, got an appointment from the French king in 1603 as lieutenant general of Acadia. He proceeded to make plans for dividing the territory of his grant, roughly from the present site of Philadelphia to Cape Breton Island, into fiefs that would be held by titled vassals dependent upon him, the lord of all *Acadie*. This division of lands he was entitled to do by the terms of the king's charter. France would profit from the fur trade, and the sovereignty of Henry IV would be extended into unknown territories. The Sieur de Monts could claim all precious metals except for a 10 percent royalty for the king. The natives were to be converted to Christianity and the northeastern American forest to a splendid European duchy ruled by a noble hierarchy with the lieutenant general at the top, answerable only to the king.

But before such a vision could be realized, there must be a very modest foothold in Acadia to serve as a base for trading and for scouting out the land and its resources. The foothold turned out to be an island in the Saint Croix River, near the present site of Calais, where du Guast and a hundred men or so camped for a miserable, scurvy-ridden fall and winter in 1604 and 1605. In the spring, the lieutenant general decided that the survivors must move or perish. In search of a new location, Samuel de Champlain, geographer to the king and one of du

Guast's principal aides, scouted the coast from the Bay of Fundy to Cape Cod. The lieutenant general himself went along with Champlain on what must have been a fine summer cruise in some of the most magnificent sailing waters in the world. It remains something of a mystery, therefore, why Champlain should have been forced to report at the end of the five-week voyage, "Sieur de Monts determined to return to the island of St. Croix, in order to find another place more favorable for our settlement, as we had not been able to do on any of the coasts which we had explored on this voyage." [6] The colony got its new start, therefore, not in Penobscot Bay or at the mouth of the Kennebec or at Richmond Island or at Cape Porpoise, all of which these two powerful and influential Frenchmen visited and described, but at Port Royal, now Annapolis, on the west coast of Nova Scotia. The remnants of the Saint Croix settlement did indeed fare better there, but in 1608 the Sieur de Monts ordered the colony abandoned because he had just lost his monopoly on the fur trade. Without that, it was clear by then, no such grand design as he had envisioned for Acadia would be possible.

Because he planted a colony at Quebec the year the Sieur de Monts's venture was abandoned, Samuel de Champlain is called the father of New France. For rather different reasons, historians conventionally regard an aristocratic English soldier with the unlikely Hispanic-sounding name of Sir Ferdinando Gorges as the father of Maine—though he himself never got there. He caught the colonizing fever while commanding the fort in the West Country port of Plymouth. This was an important job: Plymouth was England's front line of defense against a Spanish invasion in the still-dangerous years following the Armada. But by 1605, the talk of Plymouth no longer was the Spaniards, for peace had come the year before. It was America. In July of that year, Capt. George Waymouth returned to Plymouth from the scouting expedition to New England narrated in James Rosier's *Relation,* an expedition conducted for a couple of English noblemen in search of possible settlement sites. He brought with

6. Charles Herbert Levermore, ed., *Forerunners and Competitors of the Pilgrims and Puritans,* 2 vols. (Brooklyn: New England Society of Brooklyn, 1912), 1: 129.

him five Abnakis whom his crew had kidnaped near Pemaquid. For some reason we have never learned, he presented three of them to Sir Ferdinando, the "governor" of the fort. From that moment until he died forty-two years later, Gorges's life was dominated by a single passion: to sponsor colonies in the place described to him in broken English by his homesick captives.

To describe all of Sir Ferdinando's vision of New England as "feudal" would be wrong. As the young man of thirty-seven who accepted Waymouth's gift of captured Indians, his dream for colonizing America clearly belonged to the future. No English attempt to do so had yet succeeded. Gorges tried to be first by sending out a single-ship expedition in 1606 to find his Abnakis' homeland and begin a settlement, but the ship never made it and Gorges suffered a great loss. As the vigorous organizer who joined with a group that included Sir John Popham, the lord chief justice, to form the Plymouth Company, and as the middle-aged patron who in 1620 took the lead in forming the Council for New England, Gorges showed a shrewd grasp of contemporary economic realities. In the seventeenth century, it was the joint stock company that made things happen. Gorges was one of the early masters of company organization and of getting grants of land from the crown through the company structure. Moreover, throughout most of his remaining life, Gorges clung to the very practical ambition, not unlike that of his somewhat younger contemporary John Smith, to build an American colonial enterprise on fishing. But again, his luck was bad. The Popham colony at Sagadahoc, which under the sponsorship of the Council for New England had every promise of being the first permanent English settlement in America, collapsed in 1608 after only one winter in a protected sandy cove at the mouth of the Kennebec. Some of the enterprises of the Council for New England, as Gorges passed through his fifties and entered his sixties, were more successful. Not without irony, in view of Sir Ferdinando's politics and church preference, the most successful of the council's patentees by far was the Massachusetts Bay Company, whose influence in New England the aging knight spent much of the rest of his life trying unsuccessfully to resist.

Keyed to the present and to a realistic future though the plans of Gorges's middle years certainly were, the dreams that dominated the last two decades of his long life of frustration belonged entirely to a lost past. Gorges had persuaded the council to grant to him and Capt. John Mason the territory between the Merrimack and the Kennebec in 1622 and then divided his holding with Mason in 1629 to become proprietor of the "Province of Maine." In 1635, by now in his mid-sixties, Gorges conspired with Charles I to invalidate the grant of land to the Massachusetts Bay Company by a voluntary dissolution of the council for New England, which had granted it, and to make himself "lord governor" of all New England. Under his overlordship, the entire region would be divided into eight provinces, each to be held by one of the leading noblemen in the Council for New England, now dissolving. Gorges himself, besides governing the whole with the help of such officers as a bishop, a chancellor, a marshal, and an admiral, would hold one of the eight proprieties, the Province of Maine. The plan fit in nicely with certain aims of the fearsome anti-Puritan prelate, Archbishop Laud, and it appealed to the king. Gorges got his appointment and a confirmation of his grant of land, and began building a ship to take him to Maine. It was wrecked in the launching. More delays. Meanwhile, Charles's troubles with the Puritans at home came more and more to crowd out any concern with those in Massachusetts. The timing for such a grandiose scheme as Gorges's, even if the necessary settlers could have been recruited from among the English poor and the necessary money from the English rich, and even if its elaborate mechanisms had had anything at all to do with the New England reality that Gorges never saw, was all wrong. It never got off the ground.

But despite the failure of his plan for all New England, Sir Ferdinando had his Province of Maine. In 1639, he divided it, at long distance, into "bailiwicks," "hundreds," and "parishes." At the same time, he made plans to establish at Agamenticus, on the York River, the seat of an incredibly elaborate government and of a diocese of the Church of England. He sent his nephew Thomas Gorges to take charge as deputy governor. It is a merciful thing that Sir Ferdinando never got to see the thinly populated, struggling settlements over which his nephew tried valiantly to exert some kind of authority in the old proprietor's name. He died in 1647, ending half a lifetime of disappointment and an image of Maine that is more than half-forgotten.[7]

After the image of Norumbega died away, and then the visions of manorial estates that were based upon what Frenchmen and Englishmen knew about the European past rather than the American present, there remained other, more practical images. Capt. John Smith, who knew New England well, conceived of a fishermen's yeoman republic for the northeastern coast that would strengthen England morally and militarily and create a scene of simple social happiness in America. John Josselyn, a gentleman naturalist, visited America twice and spent a total of nearly ten years on the shore of Saco Bay. His image of that part of New England was that of a natural curiosity, which he reported deftly and delightfully. From Massachusetts Bay, Sir Ferdinando Gorges's province was "the eastward," the source of Indian danger, the home of rough-hewn Englishmen almost as wild as the "salvages" themselves, a potential protective buffer between the Bay Colony and Canada, and a fruitful missionary field for Puritan imperialism. Successive images continued to replace one another through the eighteenth and nineteenth and into the twentieth centuries. The process still continues.

Through all this succession of images, from the "Dawnland" through "Norumbega" and the "eastern Parts" to militant statehood and a romantic refuge from civilization, the place that Ferdinando Gorges named "Maine" remains pretty much con-

7. The most recent and convenient secondary treatment of Gorges's career is Richard Arthur Preston's *Gorges of Plymouth Fort* (Toronto: University of Toronto Press, 1953). Chapters 8–15 (pp. 137–345) deal in detail with the events summarized here. For Sir Ferdinando's own version, see his *Briefe Narration of the Originall Undertakings of Plantations into the Parts of America. Especially Shewing the Beginning, Progress and Continuance of That of New-England* (London, 1658). Reprinted as pp. 1–81 of vol. 2 of James Phinney Baxter, ed., *Sir Ferdinando Gorges and His Province of Maine*, 3 vols. (Boston: The Prince Society, 1890). Sir Ferdinando's charter of the Province of Maine, granted by Charles I in 1639, appears as pp. 123–148 of vol. 2.

stant. The curved knife-edge of Mount Katahdin, encircling a vast wooded amphitheater, rises out of the wilderness in profound isolation, separating the hills and lakes and great river valleys on the south and west from the high flatlands of Aroostook on the north and east. Sebago Lake, as it always has, changes moods in a flash from pale blue glass to fresh ripples, and then goes to dark blue and white choppy excitement and finally to gray lashing fury. The islands of Casco Bay, startling in their number and their beauty, appear and disappear from view as the fog lifts and comes in again. The sharp ledges of Pemaquid Point, bright in the summer sun, thrust out to sea and, it seems, hang breathlessly before plunging into the surging Atlantic in sight of Damarascove and Fisherman Island lying out on the west and Monhegan on the east. In places such as these the works of man seem small indeed, and the thoughts of man tend to be, in the words of the Maine poet Longfellow, "long, long thoughts."

More than most places, Maine offers a sense of permanence. What has changed over the past half-millenium, and changed often and interestingly, is the way men have thought about it. And so this bicentennial history of Maine, coming out at a time when the relationship between humanity and nature again seems a crucial thing to think about, is a history of images more than a history of a place. The fifth definition of "image" in the Oxford English Dictionary reads like this: "a mental representation of something (especially a visible object), not by direct perception, but by memory or imagination; a mental picture or impression; an idea, conception."

To write a history of Maine primarily as a state of mind may be one good way to approach a place that is hard to think about objectively. It is a peculiar place, and her people relish her—and their—peculiarities. Partly in the entirely illogical hope that this will always be so, this book is offered as a study of the successive images that have made up a special people's sense of a special place.

2

Visions Commercial, Patriotic, and Idyllic

*T*HE first images of Maine—the Dawnland, Norumbega, the feudal visions of backward-looking seigneurs and knights—belong to the Age of Discovery. The period of settlement, roughly 1610 to 1660, has its own cluster of images. They tend to be more realistic and more practical than the earlier ones, having more to do with American realities and actual possibilities. These images are a product of the settlement process itself, the beginnings of which are maddeningly fuzzy. The writings in which they appear constitute some of the most captivating literature about Maine.

Capt. John Smith, who had a seventeen-year love affair with Maine, served up in *A Description of New England* (1616) a realistic appraisal of the Maine coast. For him and for Christopher Levett, the pioneer settler of Casco Bay, the practical advantages of the region could and should have been turned to commercial profit. Smith, a man of altruistic motives as well as private ambition, considered that this kind of profit would be only a contribution to a larger goal, the glory of England. Levett shared Smith's practicality and much of his vision, but his *Voyage into New England* (1628) is less an overt expression of patriotism. On the other hand, Levett's treatment of the Maine Indians is more perceptive and sympathetic than Smith's, almost approaching the intimacy, though not the romanticism, of our third writer, John Josselyn. Josselyn, who visited the Maine coast twice in the seventeenth century, saw it primarily through the eyes of a naturalist, and his view is the most delightful of all. He gave his readers a close-up view of "rarities," both natural and political, but occasionally his science was overcome by emotion, so his two books disclose an idyllic view of Maine as well. These three images from the period of settlement—mixed with a word here and there about the settling process itself—are what this chapter is about: Smith's and Levett's commercial vision, Smith's patriotic one, and Josselyn's rarities and his idyll.

The job of actual settlement on the coast of Maine began, unsuccessfully, with Sir John Popham's colony at Sagadahoc under the sponsorship of the Council for New England. It flourished briefly in 1607–1608 and was then abandoned. It was not the Maine climate that defeated the Sagadahoc colony, nor was it disease or famine or any other failure of the place or environment. Of the forty-five colonists who passed the winter in Maine, only two died; the experiment showed conclusively that this delightful place, cold though the winter winds certainly were, could easily support human life around the year. But one of the dead was George Popham, the president of the colony. Coincidentally, two other key men died back home in England: Sir John Popham, the colony's chief sponsor, and Sir John Gilbert. That sealed the colony's fate. When Raleigh Gilbert, who succeeded George Popham as president, heard of his brother John's death, he sailed home to claim his inheritance. The remaining colonists, evidently not the best quality of prospective planters England had to offer anyway, elected to follow him.

The French made a valiant beginning in Maine as well, but that, too, was cut short. Fathers Pierre Biard and Enemond Masse, Jesuits sent in 1611 to provide a missionary presence to the Sieur de Monts's former colony at Port Royal, then owned by Jean de Poutrincourt, helped in 1613 to lead a new French colony at Mount Desert Island, even though everyone knew it was well within the English claim. Therefore, when Capt. Samuel Argall sailed from the Virginia colony into northern waters later that same year to catch fish for Jamestown, he followed the orders of Gov. Thomas Dale of Virginia to expel any French he might find within the territory claimed by England. The conquest and destruction of Saint Saveur, as the French colony was called, was swift and permanent.

This was by no means the last French gasp in Maine, but for the time being there was no effective barrier to English possession of any part of the coast, even as far east as the site of the first French settlement, which Argall also destroyed, on the Saint Croix River. As for the Abnakis, any chance of their being able to prevent an English occupation, even if they wanted to, was ended by a disastrous intertribal war between the Maine Indians and the Tarrantines, or Micmacs, of Acadia in 1614 and 1615, and an even more disastrous epidemic of smallpox that swept away thousands of native Americans from Penobscot Bay to the Narragansett country in 1617.[1]

Sometime in this period came the permanent settlement of Maine. The quest for its details is frustrating. Historians simply do not know very much about the earliest English settlement of Maine, any more than they know for sure how it got its name. Anthropologists and historical archaeologists will help someday to clear our vision of the first English settlements, but probably not even they will be able to pronounce with finality who was "first." But we do have a pretty good idea about how and why it happened.

Fishing parties from Cornwall, Dorsetshire, Somersetshire, and Devonshire began fishing the banks in the Gulf of Maine sometime around the turn of the seventeenth century. Certain islands in the very midst of the best fishing grounds— Monhegan, Damariscove, and the Isles of Shoals especially— offered obvious opportunities to go ashore, find fresh water, set up drying stages, pack the fish in casks and hogsheads for shipment, dry and repair nets, careen ships, and in general make the fishing season more efficient and comfortable than it would have been carried out entirely from ships. There were also convenient

1. For the location, identity, and spelling of the Tarrantines (called "Tarratines" in much of the literature), see Frank T. Siebert, Jr., "The Identity of the Tarrantines, with an Etymology," *Studies in Linguistics* 23 (1973): 69–79. Siebert identifies them with the Micmacs.

harbors near the ends of a few of the capes and points that stretched far enough into the ocean to be almost as handy to the best fishing as the islands were. Pemaquid was one of them, and the harbor at Sagadahoc, site of the Popham colony, was another. Cape Ann, which the Reverend John White, founder of the Dorchester Adventurers, tried to settle in 1626, seemed an obvious candidate as well. Christopher Levett reported, however, that despite its inviting harbor, "there is little good ground," and the ships that fished there in 1624 had to send their boats "twenty miles to take their Fish." [2]

By the 1620s, the ships that were gathering at these places to share the facilities and fortunes of the fishing season and to do some trading with the eastern Indians appeared not just in twos and threes but sometimes in much larger numbers. When Edward Winslow set out to the eastward from the Plymouth colony in May 1622, to seek help for the famished settlement from English fishermen, he found "above thirty sail ships" at Damariscove. Incidentally, their masters contributed as much food as they could spare. Once again, Maine had come to the rescue of Plymouth, as it had in the spring of 1621 when Samoset, who had learned his English at Pemaquid, strode into the Plymouth settlement and taught the dumbfounded Pilgrims how to survive.

Permanent colonies, John Smith and Christopher Levett and others argued eloquently, would mean that fishermen could spend a much greater share of the seven-month fishing season on the job, rather than devoting part of it to the time-consuming voyage across the Atlantic and back. Not only could more of the transatlantic voyages be devoted wholly to cargo, but ships visiting Virginia and Bermuda could touch at New England to take on fish. In the off-season, the fishermen could cultivate the fur trade with the Indians, grow some of their own food, and build permanent processing facilities, boats, and even their own ships. For just such reasons, year-round settlements began, per-

2. Christopher Levett, *A Voyage into New England Begun in 1623. and Ended in 1624.* (London, 1628), reprinted in James Phinney Baxter, *Christopher Levett, of York, the Pioneer Colonist in Casco Bay* (Portland, Me.: The Gorges Society, 1893), p. 122.

haps soon after the failure of the Popham colony, though certainly not every successful attempt at wintering-over can be considered the beginning of permanent colonization. But by 1630, the year the great Puritan migration to Massachusetts began in earnest and the year before John Smith died, there were permanent residents on the offshore islands of Monhegan, Damariscove, and the Isles of Shoals, and at nearly a dozen spots on the coast from Penobscot Bay to the Piscataqua.

This was the setting for the images of Smith, Levett, and Josselyn.

By his own account, Capt. John Smith was the most remarkable Englishman of his age. Teen-aged soldier of fortune, chivalric champion, mariner, commander of the Jamestown colony, and vigorous colonial propagandist, Smith found his way into history books as the savior of Virginia, beloved of Pocahontas. His world was far broader than that, however, as any astounded and possibly skeptical reader of his *True Travels, Adventures, and Observations* (1630) is well aware, even today.

The fact is, though it catches most readers by surprise, that the place closest to Smith's heart and imagination in the long run was the coast of Maine. In April 1614, commanding an expedition of two ships for a quartet of London merchant adventurers, Smith "chanced to arrive in *New-England,* a parte of *Ameryca,* at the Ile of *Monahigan* in 43½ of Northerly latitude." [3] A year and a half later, prisoner on board a French privateer, Smith composed his *Description of New England.* In this short tract, he reported in detail the observations and reflections of that summer's expedition, during which he had traded with the Indians and explored in detail the rivers and harbors from Penobscot Bay to Cape Cod. While he did that, most of his crew had stayed at Monhegan to carry on a summerlong fishing operation. "Of all the foure parts of the world that I have seene not inhabited," Smith wrote enthusiastically, "could I have but meanes to transport a Colonie, I would rather live here than any where: and if it did not maintaine it selfe, were

3. John Smith, *A Description of New-England* (London, 1616), reprinted in Edward Arber, ed., *The English Scholar's Library,* 5 vols. (Birmingham, England, 1878–1884; facsimile reprint, New York: AMS Press, 1967), 4–5: 187.

wee but once indifferently well fitted, let us starve." [4] Of the 400-odd miles of shoreline that Smith could have had in mind for such a colony, at least two-thirds consisted of the coast of Maine, where his crew had summered in 1614.

John Smith's image of New England, which we may with very little license translate Maine, was shaped by a pretty clear-eyed view of geographic realities and by his own strong personal traits. The image overlapped with the vision of Gorges, with whom Smith associated briefly; and in some particulars Smith's view reinforced Gorges's, but had more to do with American actualities.

Smith had been a military hero. He was a patriot, an adventurer, and an advocate and practitioner of the strenuous, dangerous life. He had devoted his career to high individual achievement. For him, the key to the honor and prosperity of England was in the founding of communities in America that would rest on a fruitful mixture of socialism and free enterprise: the communal exploitation of the rich New England fishery and the private cultivation of individually owned tracts of land. As his experience in Jamestown had shown, Smith always believed that the job of colonizing belonged only to the strong and the industrious. All others merely got in the way and ate food that they had not earned. "It is not a worke for every one," Smith wrote in *Description of New England,* "to manage such an affaire as makes a discoverie, and plants a Colony. It requires all the best parts of Art, Judgement, Courage, Honesty, Constancy, Diligence, and Industrie, to doe but neere well." [5]

The language makes us think of the Puritans: "Constancy, Diligence, and Industrie." But we mistake the matter if we think that the virtues we call "Puritan" belonged only to them. John Smith, who dedicated his *Description* to the future Charles I and a subsequent book on New England colonization to the archbishops of Canterbury and York,[6] wanted to build a plantation for the glory of God and England that would both demand

4. Smith, *Description of New-England,* Arber, 4–5: 193–194.

5. Smith, *Description of New-England,* Arber, 4–5: 191.

6. Smith, *Advertisements for the Unexperienced Planters of New-England, or any where* (London, 1631).

and exercise the strenuous virtues. For lack of opportunity and backing, he never did. That is what makes Smith's life, to whatever extent it was, a tragedy. But his vision of the sort of life that New England could provide, and what it could do for old England, stands as a moving tribute to the force of his own character and to the physical reality of the place as seen through his eyes. The main difference between his vision and that of, say, John Winthrop, first governor of Massachusetts Bay Colony, was not that Winthrop's was more practical, more moral, or even very much more pious than Smith's. It was only that Winthrop shared his vision with a large and capable audience with the means, the motivation, and a particular occasion to follow it. And he did not have all of Smith's bad luck. Whether the community Smith visualized would have survived in exactly the form he proposed is another matter, as we soon shall see. But that is not really the point, for who can argue that the Massachusetts Bay Colony survived in exactly the form proposed by John Winthrop? The fact is that the Bay Colony did survive and prosper in *some* form; given similar advantages, a colony based on Smith's vision might have done equally well.

"The maine Stapel," Smith wrote, ". . . is fish." Thus he began the job of fashioning a vision of a future society with a realistic appraisal of the place itself. His argument for founding the economy of New England upon fishing, "however it may seeme a mean and a base commoditie," was a compound of patriotism and shrewdness. At the time of writing, the only permanent English settlement in America was the still-shaky one at Jamestown, which Smith had left in other hands in 1609. English assumptions about the pre-eminent source of national wealth—and thus the main attraction in colonies—were the same in the first two decades of the seventeenth century as they had been throughout the spectacularly successful "Spanish century," just now dying. The mercantile theory called for hard money, and the most obvious source of that was in mines of silver and gold. Smith's answer to this assumption was to shift his countrymen's attention from their old enemies, the Spaniards, to their chief commercial rivals, the Dutch.

The "Hollanders," Smith argued, are made "hardy and industrious" by the challenge of deep-sea fishing in all weather. By selling "this poore commodity" in southern Europe, they are made "mighty, strong, and rich." Smith then compared the riches of the Dutch and the Spaniards: "And never could the Spaniard with all his Mynes of golde and Silver pay his debts, his friends, and army, halfe so truly, as the Hollanders still have done by this contemptible trade of fish. . . . This is their Myne; and the Sea the source of those silvered streames of all their vertue; which hath made them now the very miracle of industrie." [7]

The lesson for England, of course, was that there were plenty of fish in American waters ready for the taking, and that these teeming fishing grounds were astonishingly close to the great forests of New England, "where there is victuall to feed us, wood of all sorts to build Boats, Ships, or Barks; the fish at our doores; pitch, tarre, masts, yards, and most of other necessaries only for making." Moreover, land was abundant, and it beckoned to the more imaginative and courageous citizens of an overpopulated, dissipated, idle England.

Fish and land. The one would enrich the nation, the other the individual.

A beneficent deity had placed stores of unlikely riches in the best part of the American territory that England had long since claimed, the part that Smith himself christened "New England." By mining these riches of sea and earth instead of going in futile search of gold and silver, the English could undercut the Dutch trade with southern Europe, bring wealth to the nation, rid the realm of some of its surplus population, harden the bodies and character of a soft generation, and train sailors and build ships for the eventual use of a crown whose power and dignity would rest henceforth upon control of the seas.

These "new" Englanders would not be fishermen only, but fishermen-farmers. Smith's vision was not tied to a single working arrangement, but one possible model would involve great companies of men, a hundred or so, each working for an hour or two each day in the communal fishery. Thus they would

---

7. Smith, *Description of New-England,* Arber, 4–5: 193–194.

"make their provision for a day." For the rest of the day each man would be free to work his own land. Another model would have smaller companies of "industrious men" employed practically full time under able managers to defend and feed the larger community of gentlemen, craftsmen, and householders, presumably for wages. However organized such a community might be, the attraction in joining it would be the opportunity to tap unlimited resources at small financial cost but at some hazard to life and limb.

The very risks of colonization appealed to Smith as an ennobling experience, good alike for individual and country:

> Who can desire more content, that hath small meanes; or but only his merit to advance his fortune, then to tread, and plant that ground hee hath purchased by the hazard of his life? If he have but a taste of virtue and magnanimitie, what to such a minde can be more pleasant, then planting and building a foundation for his Posteritie, gotte from the rude earth, by Gods blessing and his own industrie, without prejudice to any? [8]

Here is almost an early version, given a more tangy flavor than the later one by the smell of salt spray and curing fish, of Thomas Jefferson's famous argument for the moral advantages of farming that produced his vision of the yeoman republic.

Actual experience in seventeenth-century New England cast some doubt upon the workability of Smith's idea of the fisherman-farmer. The Reverend Mr. White of the Dorchester Adventurers tried out a version of Smith's idea in an unsuccessful effort to settle the Massachusetts North Shore in 1626. He found that "No sure fishing place in the land is fit for planting nor any good place for planting found fit for fishing, at least near the shore. And, secondly, rarely any fishermen will work at land, neither are husbandmen fit for fishermen but with long use and experience." [9]

Nevertheless, Smith was both serious and enthusiastic, and

8. Smith, *Description of New-England,* Arber, 4–5: 208.

9. Charles M. Andrews, *The Colonial Period of American History,* 4 vols. (New Haven: Yale University Press, 1934–1938), 1: 351, quoted in A. L. Rowse, *The Elizabethans and America* (London: Macmillan & Co., 1959), p. 113.

the saltwater farms of eighteenth- and nineteenth-century Maine, although they were hardly integrated parts of the close colonial communities that Smith visualized, demonstrated that the idea of combining farming and fishing in some way was not as farfetched in the long run as contemporary experience seemed to suggest.

The rest of Smith's argument in a half-dozen books and pamphlets is little more than elaboration, and the rest of his career, alas, too quickly told. Back in England from his voyage of 1614, Smith sought out Sir Ferdinando Gorges, who himself had just been disappointed by the failure of one of the many ventures he had tried to sponsor in the region that Smith was now calling New England. Sir Ferdinando sold Smith's vision to the Plymouth Company, which then made Smith "Admiral of New England" and, with the help of some outside backing, assembled an expedition of two ships. The plan was for the expedition to leave the core of a colony—seventeen settlers with Smith at the head—at some spot in New England to await a relief ship and reinforcements a year later. The two ships sailed early in 1615, aiming to rendezvous at Monhegan. Smith's ship, crippled by Atlantic storms, had to hobble back to Plymouth under a jury rig. Gorges found another ship, in which Smith and his company sailed from Plymouth on June 24, 1615, but French pirates captured her near the Azores. While Smith was negotiating with his captors on board one of the French ships, his own mutinous crew slipped away and sailed home to England. It was during the depressing, humiliating voyage to France as prisoner in a foreign vessel that Smith wrote *A Description of New-England*.

Back in England yet another time, Smith got his manuscript published, visited John Rolfe and his bride Pocahontas, newly arrived in London from Virginia, and secured the backing of a merchant coalition for another try at colonization in 1617. This time, his three ships (originally he had been promised twenty) were kept in Plymouth Harbor for three months by a southwest gale. When the wind was finally right, it was too late in the season to sail, and then his backers called the expedition off. By now Smith and Gorges, two strong conflicting personalities, were developing a mutual distrust, and Gorges had begun putting his hopes for Maine in other hands. Smith offered his services as military commander to the Plymouth Pilgrims in 1620, but they, probably wisely, chose Miles Standish instead. From then until his death in June 1631 at the age of 51, Smith devoted himself to propagating his vision of American colonization and to vindicating himself. In the books that resulted,[10] we have the beginnings of an American literature and the disclosure of a fascinating mind and personality. We also find in most of those books a repetition and occasional embellishment of the vision he described first in *Description of New England*. To the modern reader, his vision is a tragic one because it glimpses a society that might have been, but never was, on the coast of Maine.

While Smith spent his waning years in propagandizing and in the frustrating quest for further backing, the actual work of settling Maine began—without flamboyance, without publicity, without vast sums of money, and, to the despair of the modern historian, without much in the way of records. It is somewhat discomforting to those of us who write for a living to discover that those who wrote the most and best about their experiences are not likely to have been the ones with the most successful experiences. One of those who tried valiantly to colonize, like John Smith, was a vigorous and ingenious English gentleman named Christopher Levett. In 1623 and 1624, he tried to make a colony at Casco Bay. Like Smith and Popham, he failed. But when he sailed home in 1624 expecting vainly to return, he left behind ten colonists who may have joined one or more of the other settlements that were now beginning. Another result of his attempt was a fascinating account of his travels on the Maine coast. This little book, *A Voyage into New England,* published in London in 1628, tells us a good deal about the English and the Indians in Maine in the mid-1620s, and it reinforces Smith's

---

10. *New Englands Trials* (London, 1620; 1622); *The Generall Historie of Virginia, New-England, and the Summer Isles* (London, 1624); *An Accidence or The Path-way to Experience. Necessary for all Young Seamen* (London, 1626); *The True Travels, Adventures, and Observations of Captaine John Smith* (London, 1630); *Advertisements for the Unexperienced Planters* (London, 1631).

vision of the Maine coast by offering similar arguments for its settlement.

Christopher Levett was a naval captain, a member of the Council for New England, and the woodward of the royal forests in Somersetshire. In this last capacity, he looked after the king's mast trees and pioneered in compiling tables for measuring lumber. In 1623, the council granted him 6,000 acres within the Gorges-Mason territory. Acquiring a ship, some prospective settlers, and money to build a fort at a place he proposed to name ''York'' after his native city, Levett sailed for New England that summer. His ship, carrying part of his prospective colony, arrived at the Isles of Shoals in the autumn; others of his men had shipped passage on various fishing and trading vessels to numerous points on the Maine coast. For a month he gathered his scattered group together while staying with David Thomson, who had begun a settlement the same year at Odiorne's Point on the New Hampshire side of the Piscataqua. Then, in the stormy and chill weather of late autumn, made even worse than usual by unseasonably early snowstorms, he took all of his men in two boats to explore the coast to the east.

A Voyage into New England provides a valuable and detailed description of the lower Maine coast, including its native inhabitants and its English sojourners, from the Piscataqua to the Boothbay region. Levett lost one of his men in a storm off Saco, but aside from sickness and severe discomfort from chill and dampness, his company apparently suffered no other casualties. His account of the two little boats being tossed at sea and lost in the fog between Saco and Cape Porpoise, however, cannot help but stir sympathetic reactions from any who have ever been caught in Maine waters under similar circumstances:

> . . . before we could recover the harbour a great fog of mist tooke us that we could not see a hundred yards from us. I perceiving the fog to come upon the Sea, called for a Compasse and set the Cape land, by which wee knew how to steare our course, which was no sooner done but wee lost sight of land, and my other boate, and the winde blew fresh against us, so that we were enforced to strike saile and betake us to our Oares which wee used with all the wit and

strength we had, but by no meanes could we recover the shore that night, being imbayed and compassed round with breaches, which roared in a most fearfull manner on every side of us. . . . At length I caused our Killick [a small anchor, probably made of a rock] . . . to be cast forth, and one continually to hold his hand upon the . . . cable, by which we knew whether our ancker held or no: which being done wee commended our selves to God by prayer, & put on a resolution to be as comfortable as we could, and so fell to our victuals. Thus we spent that night, and the next morning, with much adoe we got into Sawco, where I found my other boate.[11]

For his settlement of "York," Levett chose one of the most obvious sites on the coast, unaccountably overlooked by Sieur de Monts, Champlain, and John Smith. The local Indians called it "Quack"; at least that is how Levett tried to render it for his English readers. The territory encompassed all the islands in Portland Harbor and the nearby parts of Casco Bay; his grant of 6,000 acres extended to a big piece of the mainland as well, probably including what later became Falmouth Neck and the modern city of Portland. The best guess is that Levett built his fortified trading house and future fishing station on House Island. Having laid the foundation of his colony with the building, and after establishing friendly relations with several nearby sagamores, he sailed home in the summer of 1624 to get more money and to rejoin his family, with whom he expected to return shortly to Maine. His account of his last encounter with the Indian leaders is both revealing and touching:

They asked me why I would be gone out of their Countrey, I was glad to tell them my wife would not come thither except I did fetch her, they bid a pox on her hounds (a phrase they have learned and doe use when they doe curse) and wished me to beate her. I told them no, for then our God would bee angrie. Then they runne out upon her in evil tearmes, and wished me to let her alone and take another, I told them our God would be more angrie for that. Againe they bid me beate her, beate her, repeating it often, and very angerly, but I answered no, that was not the English fashion, and besides, she was a good wife and I had children by her, and I loved her well, so I satisfied them. Then they told me that I and my wife

11. Levett, *A Voyage into New England*, pp. 93–94.

and Children, with all my friends, should bee hartily welcome into that Countrey at any time.[12]

Levett, though not nearly as well known as the colorful Smith, shared a similar view of Maine and its possibilities, expressed it more concisely, and came far closer to realizing the schemes that his vision of the place inspired. In 1628 (February 1627 Old Style), after several futile attempts to gain orders and backing from the preoccupied court of Charles I, Levett finally got some encouragement. One of England's more ill-considered wars with France had broken out in 1626. Levett proposed to lead a fleet of four ships to New England. There he would drive the French fishermen from the banks, protect English shipping from the French and the Spaniards, with whom England was then also at war, consolidate English activities in the region with a view both to defense and commercial profit, and at the risk of his own money, resume his colony at "York." This fine harbor, besides serving as headquarters for his own enterprises, could provide an important public service, namely, the storage of all the English fishing shallops on the coast during the off-season under Levett's protection. The king and council, moved by the military advantages of the scheme and, so the proclamation said, the opportunity to convert the Maine Indians to Christianity, ordered a collection taken up in every parish church for the support of Levett's plan.

In the same year, evidently to encourage generous contributions in the parishes of the realm, Levett published his *Voyage into New England*. The book, like the writings of Smith, urges the colonization of New England for the glory of God and of England. Like John Josselyn who followed him, Levett was a keen observer of the Indians. He was not, however, nearly the moralist that Smith was, nor the detailed and comprehensive naturalist that produced Josselyn's nicely catalogued observations. Levett saw Maine primarily with a view to profits; the means would be the now-familiar fish and timber. Where Smith's argument tended to be passionate, Levett's was coolly

12. Levett, *A Voyage into New England,* pp. 111–112.

logical. To answer doubts and objections, he simply summoned the best evidence he could find in rebuttal; to nail down his promise of profits, he offered calculations in pounds, shillings, and pence.

Yes, he admitted to those who feared that English colonists would starve in New England, Thomas Weston's men had failed from hunger at Weymouth in 1622–1623, but that was because they had spent the best planting and fishing time building forts instead of laying in food. And another Englishman, one Chapman, who had come alone to Plymouth with two servants, may indeed have starved to death. But that was because he had daily sold off part of the eighteen-month supply of provisions he had brought in order to spend "seven or eight pound a week in wine, Tobacco, and whores." [13]

To those who argued that colonizing schemes were aimed at the private good of their sponsors but the detriment of the country, Levett offered some of the familiar responses of Smith, but then went on to try to prove them with figures. Through a complex reasoning process, Levett demonstrated that a crew of fifty men sent to fish and live in a colony in Maine could return £2,680 on an investment of £1,066.13.4, as opposed to a return of £1,340 on £800 invested in the same number of men sent to fish during the season and brought home again. In support of the parish contributions then being solicited, he pleaded that each parish "adventure so much as they pay weekly to the reliefe of the poore," and that each shire send "men to plant." John Smith would have rested his plea on the long-term fiscal, military, and moral advantages of providing strenuous, adventurous work for idle people. Levett, shrewder and more practical, added a promise of an immediate return on the investment. After eighteen months, the profit to each parish should be sufficient to "keep their poore, and ease their purses"—provided each shire's quota of settlers was accompanied by an able leader. If there is no such profit, Levett boasted, "will I be contented to suffer death." [14]

13. Levett, *A Voyage into New England*, pp. 126–127.
14. Levett, *A Voyage into New England*, p. 136.

Levett died all right, and not long afterward, but not in connection with the flamboyant gesture by which he tried to encourage the parish collections. The collections, in fact, though they were taken up in due course, fell short of what was needed to do the job. Levett never carried out his scheme; the Maine sagamores awaited his return to Casco Bay in vain. In 1629 or 1630, Levett did command a ship to Salem, where he conferred with John Winthrop when the Puritan fleet arrived in Massachusetts Bay. He died at sea, aged forty-four, during the voyage home in 1630.

By that time, the settlement of New England was progressing smartly. Levett, like Smith, had failed to lead a settlement on the Maine coast. Sir Ferdinando Gorges was still full of hopes and dreams for New England, not yet realizing—if he ever did—that the real future of the region lay with the earnest middle-class men and women then populating Salem and Boston. Still, the fishing and trading settlements from the Piscataqua to Pemaquid were thriving in their limited fashion, and more such colonies were being added almost yearly in the 1630s.

On the third of July 1638, John Josselyn, son of Sir Thomas Josselyn of Essex, who was a councillor for the Province of Maine under Gorges, arrived in Boston Harbor aboard the ship *New Supply*. It is unclear whether his father, too, may have been on board. Most of the 160 passengers were joining the stream of 3,000 emigrants who during that summer alone were fleeing the schemes and fulminations of Anglican Archbishop William Laud to join Governor Winthrop's Puritan mission in Massachusetts. But not John Josselyn. He and old Sir Thomas, if he was there, had come to pay a visit to Henry, Sir Thomas's elder son, on the coast of Maine. Henry had been in America for four years. Most recently he had been an employee of Gorges, and briefly a member of the Maine government, such as it was, at Black Point in the modern town of Scarborough.

John Josselyn, who was probably about thirty years old when he made his first trip to America, sailed home to England fifteen months later. His life for the next twenty-four years is an utter blank as far as any record is concerned, but in the spring of

1663 he accepted an invitation from Henry to come to Maine again. This time, he stayed at Black Point nearly eight and a half years. Before he died in 1675, home in England, he published two books about his experiences and observations in New England. In those two books, *New-Englands Rarities Discovered* (1672) and *An Account of Two Voyages to New-England* (1674, second edition, 1675), are contained virtually everything we know about this remarkable naturalist, delightful author, bon vivant, and, one cannot help but suspect, occasional liar.

Though it is evident from Josselyn's exuberant character that he must have packed much more into his sixty-seven years or so than appears on the record, his world as he described it consisted entirely of two round-trip voyages and about ten years on the coast of Maine. That much was a wonderful world, indeed, observed through eyes that were at once amused and fascinated, and described by the deft, often droll, pen of a cultivated Restoration writer.

The coast from Boston to Scarborough as he saw it during his first visit was "no other than a meer Wilderness, here and there by the Seaside a few scattered plantations, with as few houses." [15] The woods, however, if one accepts the full implications of his account, literally teemed with creatures he delighted in naming and describing. The porcupine, which could grow "as big as an ordinary mungrel cur," laid eggs and defended itself, he believed, by "shooting a whole shower of quills" at its enemies. The pond frogs "chirp in the spring like sparrows, and croke like toads in autumn." Some, "when they set upon their breech, are a foot high." The distinctive weapon of the "Squnck" was its urine, of a strong lasting scent and "so sharp that if he do but whisk his bush which he pisseth upon in the face of a dogg . . . and that any of it light in his eyes it will make him almost mad with the smart thereof." The full-grown moose was "many times bigger than an English oxe." "The Bear when he goes to mate is a terrible Creature," and both the

15. John Josselyn, *An Account of Two Voyages to New-England Made During the Years 1638, 1663* (reprint of London, 1675 ed.; Boston: W. Veazie, 1865), p. 20.

fox and the wolf "go a clicketing the beginning of the spring, and bring forth their Cubs in May and June." [16]

Josselyn obviously had had some medical training. He put heavy emphasis upon the curative properties of the plants and animals he collected and described, and reported that he actually worked some cures in New England, among both Indians and whites. He was enthusiastic about the medicinal qualities of many New England plants, but over none did he grow quite so poetic as he did over tobacco, of which the Maine Indians raised an inferior variety. "The vertues of Tobacco," wrote Josselyn, "are these,"

> it helps digestion, the Gout, the Tooth-ach, prevents infection by scents, it heats the cold, and cools them that sweat, feedeth the hungry, spent spirits restoreth, purgeth the stomach, killeth nits and lice; the juice of the green leaf healeth green wounds, although poysoned; the Syrup for many diseases, the smoak for the Phthisick, cough of the lungs, distillations of Rheume, and all diseases of a cold and moist cause, good for all bodies cold and moist taken upon an emptie stomach, taken upon a full stomach it precipitates digestion.

Not even so marvelous a sovereign as this could be entirely free from ill effects, and Josselyn was quick to acknowledge it. "Immoderately taken," he admitted, "it dryeth the body, enflameth the bloud, hurteth the brain, weakens the eyes and the sinews." [17]

English housewives in Maine had already learned how to cook tasty dishes out of the native New England vegetables. From "pompions," or pumpkins, they made what Josselyn called "The ancient New-England standing Dish," for which he thoughtfully provided the recipe:

> . . . slice them when ripe, and cut them into dice, and so fill a pot with them of two or three gallons and stew them upon a gentle fire a

16. Josselyn, *New-Englands Rarities Discovered* (London, 1672; pp. 152, 168. Reprinted in *American Antiquarian Society Transactions* 4 [1860]); *An Account of Two Voyages,* pp. 67–75.

17. Josselyn, *An Account of Two Voyages,* pp. 61–62.

whole day; and, as they sink . . . fill again with fresh pompions, not putting any liquor to them; and, when it is stew'd enough, it will look like bak'd apples. This they dish; putting butter to it, and a little vinegar (with some spice, as ginger, &c); which makes it tart, like an apple; and so serve it up, to be eaten with fish or flesh. It provokes urin extreamly, and is very windy.[18]

Nowadays, the "ancient New-England standing Dish" is put in a pie crust and served after turkey instead of with it.

Besides being fascinated by the flora and fauna of the Maine coast, Josselyn found quickly that human company there, though sparse, could be both interesting and congenial. During his first visit to Scarborough in 1638, he reveled in the company of "neighboring gentlemen," who came to Henry's house to welcome the visitor to America and told marvelous tall stories. The stories were all Gothic tales of the sea, whether they dealt with a merman who oozed purple blood when his hand was chopped off, a sea serpent "quoiled up like a Cable upon a Rock," or a band of ghostly Indians who called a seaman's name from the shore at night but disappeared when the seaman landed on the beach in the morning. Josselyn dutifully reported them all to his readers with the laconic observation, "There are many stranger things in the world than are to be found between London and Stanes." [19]

Some of these visitors may have come from Richmond Island, just off modern Cape Elizabeth, where about sixty male employees of Robert Trelawney of Plymouth, England, worked at a fishing and trading station that had been set up in 1632 by Trelawney's agent, John Winter. Winter reported to Trelawney the year Josselyn returned to England the first time that in Gorges's Maine, "every man is a law to him selfe. Yt is a bad kind of livinge to live in a place where is neather law nor government amonge people." [20]

Josselyn never complained about that, except to criticize the

18. Josselyn, *New-Englands Rarities,* pp. 224–225.

19. Josselyn, *An Account of Two Voyages,* pp. 22–23.

20. James Phinney Baxter, ed., "Trelawney Papers," *Documentary History of Maine,* 24 vols. (Portland, 1869–1916), 3:171.

Massachusetts authorities, who had managed to take charge of Maine before he returned the second time. He may have been a bit taken aback but nevertheless touched and pleased when at six o'clock on the morning of his departure, "several of my friends came to bid me farewell, among the rest Captain Thomas Wannerton who drank to me a pint of kill-devil alias Rhum at a draught." [21]

As for the English settlers who were beneath the station of the Josselyns, they got scant respect from the writer. The farmers were of a "droanish disposition," he complained, and the fishermen too often drunk.

However restrained his reactions to the English settlers in Maine, Josselyn was greatly impressed with the natural virtues and skills of the local Indians, whom he evidently came to know well. He wrote in detail of their hunting and fishing practices, their recipes, and their family life. He deplored instances of their debauchery by English vices. He despised their religious beliefs and superstitions and their cruelty in warfare, but he admired their cleverness, their friendship, and their bravery. And, though he found the men "somewhat horse-fac'd," he admired their women.

One of New England's "rarities," surely, was—and is—the Maine lobster. But Josselyn was even more impressed with what the Saco Bay Indians did with them than by the creatures themselves. At low tide, he reported, Indian boys would go out into large bays in birch canoes "with a staff two or three yards long, made small and sharpen'd at one end, and nick'd with deep nicks to take hold. When they spye the Lobster crawling upon the Sand in two fathom water, more or less, they stick him towards the head and bring him up. I have known thirty Lobsters taken by an Indian lad in an hour and a half." [22] They cooked them mainly by baking.

The Indian women were hard-working, uncomplaining, and "have the easiest labours of any women in the world." When their time came, they simply took a two-foot board with them

21. Josselyn, *An Account of Two Voyages,* p. 24.
22. Josselyn, *An Account of Two Voyages,* p. 109.

into the woods, lay down next to a tree or a bush, and "are delivered in a trice, not so much as groaning for it." Next "they
wrap the child up in a young Beaver-skin with his heels close to
his britch, leaving a little hole if it be a Boy for his Cock to
peep out at; and lace him down to the board upon his back, his
knees resting upon the foot beneath, then putting the strap of
leather upon their fore-head with the infant hanging at their
back, home they trudge." [23]

Josselyn, however, was not simply a detached observer of Indian women. Just how well he knew them is best judged by the
little compliment to the "Indian squa" with which he ended
New-Englands Rarities. The Indian women, he sighed, "have
very good features; seldom without a come-to-me, or *cos
amoris,* in their countenance; . . . broad-breasted; handsome,
streight bodies, and slender . . . ; their limbs cleanly, straight,
and of a convenient stature,—generally as plump as partridges;
and, saving here and there one, of a modest deportment." Modest they have been, but Josselyn was so taken by their other
assets that he closed his report with some verses:

> Whether white or black be best,
> Call your senses to the quest;
> And your touch shall quickly tell,
> The black in softness doth excel,
> And in smoothness: but the ear—
> What! can that a colour hear?
> No, but 'tis your black one's wit
> That doth catch and captive it.
>
> . . . .
>
> And such perfection here appears,
> It neither wind nor sunshine fears. [24]

The year John Josselyn died, the outbreak of King Philip's
War effectively spelled the end of the peaceful, idyllic relations
that apparently Josselyn visualized between the English and the
Indians in Maine. Hostilities between the races deepened during
the series of intercolonial wars that extended from 1689 to 1763

---

23. Josselyn, *An Account of Two Voyages,* pp. 99–100.
24. Josselyn, *New-Englands Rarities,* pp. 231–232.

and became almost the definitive feature of the northern New England experience in the eighteenth century. The writings of John Josselyn, in addition to their other uses, provide a glimpse of what, in the most uninhibited corner of New England, might otherwise have been.

Images. John Smith's image of Maine was heroic, Christopher Levett's commercial. Josselyn's? Analytical and genteel, certainly, and almost scientific. But in addition it was a version of the old European quest for an earthly paradise, Eden before the Fall. There is not much of that in the literature of Massachusetts, except perhaps for the writings of the renegade Thomas Morton. But for a brief moment, John Josselyn thought he had found a place of innocence, pleasure, and biracial happiness on the coast of Maine.

3

Eastward into the Desert

*O*F all Boston divines, Cotton Mather remains the most famous. He flourished during that tumultuous time when seventeenth-century faith was fading into eighteenth-century reason, and it was not always possible to separate the two. It was a time of superstition and of science, and Mather indulged in both. It was the time of witches, of political upheaval in old England and new, and of fearsome Indian wars that devastated the outlying settlements and kept Boston on nervous guard. Cotton Mather spent his life fighting a last-ditch action to keep the religious, social, and political life of his province in the same kind of hands that had held it during the generations of his father and his grandfather, as eminent in their own times as Cotton Mather was in his. It was, in the end, a losing cause. But it was a glorious fight. And in the course of its many battles, Mather's prolific pen sketched, among other things, a comprehensive ideology of conquest aimed specifically at the wild sprawling territory that lay to the northeast of Massachusetts Bay. As this ideology begins to take shape in the modern reader's mind from a perusal of several of Mather's writings, we realize that his image of Maine, an image that justified a conquest that had already taken place and provided an instrument for its further refinement, was a far cry indeed from the heroic vision of Smith, the commercial vision of Levett, and especially the idyllic vision of Josselyn.

Cotton Mather thought of Maine as a desert.

"I am to lead you this day thro' a spacious country which has been on many accounts the most charming part of New-England," he wrote in 1698. Yet, he added, "I must herewithal say, 'come, behold the works of the Lord, what desolations he has made in that land.' " [1] It was Maine, along with coastal New Hampshire, that Mather was describing as the once-charming but now desolate land. In a lecture to his Boston congregation, delivered near the end of the decade-long War of the League of Augsburg (known in America as King William's War), Mather tried to set forth the moral and religious lesson of that devastating conflict. The lesson was important enough for the lecture to take an honored place indeed: it was enshrined in print as the last several pages of Mather's greatest work, *Magnalia Christi Americana,* that curious monumental history of New England published in 1702.

The killing and the destruction had been on the eastern frontier, where the boundary between Acadia and New England was always in contest and where Abnakis converted to the leadership and religion of France could be used as willing shock troops in the long Anglo-French struggle for European dominance and American empire. Nearly every settlement in Maine, from the fortified outpost at Pemaquid on the extreme frontier to Berwick, York, and Kittery, together with the Dover and Oyster River settlements in New Hampshire, had suffered from quick, fatal raids. Hundreds of houses had been burned and more than 700 Maine settlers either killed or taken prisoner to Canada. East of Wells, the best-defended settlement in Maine, all the former English villages had been abandoned.

Why had all this happened? Mather had an answer for most things, and this was no exception. The eastern settlements had had practically no churches! The presence of a church and an evangelical minister had served as the best protection against French and Indian raiders. That was obvious since not one town that had been utterly destroyed and abandoned in the war had had either, and every town that had enjoyed these Protestant blessings had been spared complete destruction.

Think of it! Plantations without churches, founded perhaps

1. *Magnalia Christi Americana,* 2 vols. (Hartford: Silas Andrus, 1820), 2:573.

for fishing or for trading, but not for the advancement of the gospel according to the Winthrops, the Cottons, and the Mathers. Here on the very edges of the new Canaan, divinely set aside as the home of the new Chosen People, was a spiritual wasteland, a kind of Sinai Desert set between the New English Israelites and the hopeless sensuality and superstition of the Egypt that was New France. The proposition that the fishermen and lumbermen of Maine belonged properly within the saving remnant of New England may have been more obvious to Cotton Mather than to the Maine settlers themselves. But no matter. As strayed, or perhaps as yet untaught brethren, they needed the chastisement of the Lord to set their way straight. And just as he had used the Philistines of old to correct his chosen Israel, God was now using heathens and papists to correct people who, whether they knew it or not (suffice it that Cotton Mather knew) belonged truly to Him—which is to say they belonged to Mather's New England. They had acted like pagans, or at least so it seemed from the perspective of Boston. "For this cause we may believe it is," proclaimed Mather, "that our Lord Jesus Christ looking down from Heaven upon these unchristian undertakings, thunder-struck them with his indignation." [2] Mather acknowledged almost reluctantly that the "eastern country" would soon be settled again. This time, it was clear, repeated destruction could be avoided in only one way: "Let the people which intend there to settle themselves in the fear of God, remember this admonition; don't venture to form *towns* without the *gospel* in them any more." [3]

Nine years before his Boston lecture of 1698, Mather had made his image of the desert even more explicit. In 1689, King William's War had just broken out between the English and the French and Mather was exhorting a group of Massachusetts militiamen who were on their way to fight the "eastern Indians" of Maine. Physically, the land beyond the Piscataqua may indeed have been "charming," a word that crept into the lecture of 1698. But like most Puritan writers, Mather did not

2. *Magnalia*, 2:574.
3. *Magnalia*, 2:575.

concern himself primarily with the natural state of things—unless it was to identify "remarkable providences" that might contain special signals from God. Far more important to him was the moral landscape. That was a dreary place indeed, for which the soldiers who were about to enter it needed special preparation and sustenance. He told the soldiers of 1689 that by carrying with them "Gods Laws . . . in your Minds," they would have nourishment "for the Repast of your Souls in the Desert which you range forth into." This would compensate for the unpleasant fact that, as Mather said, "You cannot always come at those Ordinances, which are the Wells of Salvation, being driven to wander in the Dry paths of a Solitary Wilderness." [4]

Cotton Mather's image of a desert, or "solitary wilderness," was nothing new. Puritan ministers, soldiers, and governors in the generations of his father Increase and grandfather Richard may not usually have evoked quite as vivid a picture of the reality they had seen to the northeast of Massachusetts. But they had been equally certain that such an ungodly place was sorely in need of their attention. It needed to be rescued from the Indians, from the French, from the Devil, and from those whom Cotton Mather called the "wild English." The men of Massachusetts looked upon the rescue operation as a good work, but could hardly ignore the fact that the possession of Maine would also be to the benefit of their own trade and their own defense. Out of such concerns grew the first American imperialism.

Massachusetts imperialism, to give it a harsh but accurate name, began in one sense even before there was a Massachusetts Bay Colony. In 1622, Edward Winslow and his crew from the Plymouth colony had got help from the English fishermen at Damariscove. The Pilgrims kept up their contacts with the Maine coast every summer thereafter and came to know its coves, harbors, and river mouths well. Then in 1625, after the best harvest ever, Winslow and some companions took a shallop load of surplus Plymouth corn up the Kennebec and traded it to willing Indians along the river for 700 pounds of beaver skins.

4. *Souldiers Counselled and Comforted* (Boston: Samuel Green [1689]), p. 14.

Here began the pattern of trade that eventually bailed out the Pilgrims from their heavy indebtedness to their English sponsors. By 1628, the Plymouth men had found a way to get Massachusetts wampum from neighboring Indians and used that, along with some trading stock they brought from a failing colony at Monhegan, to acquire the precious furs at a permanent, fortified truck house at the present site of Augusta. They built the house after the Council for New England made the colony a grant of land on both sides of the Kennebec in 1629. By then, however, Thomas Morton, the merry vagabond and leader of the famous band of rowdies at Merry Mount (now Quincy, Massachusetts), had discovered the possibility of making riches in Maine and had begun a serious competitive operation there featuring an even more attractive payment to the Kennebec Indians—liquor and gunpowder. Morton was soon overcome and sent back to England, and the profit in beaver continued to mount. A tradition of expansion and competition for markets had generated from the shores of Massachusetts Bay even before the arrival in Salem and Boston of the main body of settlers that came to dominate the colony. The Kennebec operation became the envy of other prospective English traders. One of them, John Hocking of Piscataqua, provoked a nasty incident in 1634 when he tried to force a vessel up the river past the Pilgrim trading post to intercept the Indian trappers with his own goods before they reached Augusta. Hocking shot first, killing one of the Plymouth men, and he was killed in return before his expedition retreated downriver.

Eventually, despite its very real early successes, the Kennebec venture became less profitable and more hazardous. In 1661, Plymouth colony sold its Maine land to four Boston merchants for £400.

The sale of the Kennebec lands to a Boston-based combination of long-term investors was symptomatic of what was happening throughout Maine, and indeed throughout much of New England: The region was coming gradually but inexorably under the control of the Massachusetts Bay Colony. This was a form of imperialism—political, religious, commercial, and even military—that responded in various ways to the image that Cotton

Mather finally articulated in the 1690s. It brought Massachusetts soldiers and diplomats, merchants, and missionaries trooping earnestly eastward into the desert they wanted to reclaim for God and for profit.

The main body of the Puritan company under John Winthrop that really began the Massachusetts Bay Colony in 1630 lost little time in extending its own brand of politics and religion beyond the boundaries of its own patent. Expansion began by migration into Connecticut in 1636, by banishment of religious dissidents to Rhode Island and New Hampshire at about the same time, and by a variegated and thorough movement, with only temporary results, to take over the four towns of New Hampshire between 1637 and 1643.

The conquest of Maine was more complicated and more permanent. Not only did the traders of Plymouth and Massachusetts Bay continue their profitable relationship with the Indians in the Sagadahoc country through the 1640s and 1650s, but they discovered in the middle of the seventeenth century that there was also a profit to be made from the lonely English fishermen who sailed out of their tiny stations from the Isles of Shoals to Monhegan Island and Pemaquid. During his second visit to Scarborough in the 1660s, John Josselyn was fascinated by the trading barks from Massachusetts that called at the fishing colonies at the peak of the season to work their trade. These "walking taverns," as he called them, would dispense to the fishermen "a Taster or two, which so charms them, that for no perswasions that their imployers can use will they go out to Sea . . . for two or three days, nay sometimes a whole week till they are wearied with drinking, taking ashore two or three Hogsheads of *Wine* and *Rhum* to drink off when the Merchant is gone." [5]

Political and commercial imperialism prospered together. From 1649 to 1660, Puritans ruled in England instead of kings, and colonial affairs were never more remote. Massachusetts was free to follow her tendency toward independence and expansion

5. John Josselyn, *An Account of Two Voyages to New-England Made During the Years 1638, 1663* (Boston: W. Veazie, 1865), p. 161.

unrestrained. Between 1650 and 1658, following a homemade interpretation of the Massachusetts charter that placed its northern boundary in the middle of Casco Bay, the Bible Commonwealth went to work on the absorption of Maine. Commissioners from the general court visited every settlement between the Piscataqua and Casco Bay, aiming to fill what was really a political vacuum.

Due to a succession of confusing circumstances, there was actually very little government. Sir Ferdinando Gorges's Province of Maine had been divided into two proprieties in 1630; his deputy Thomas Gorges was away in England; Sir Ferdinando and Sir Alexander Rigby, proprietor of the northern half of the province (called Lygonia), both died in 1647; and there was a factional feud in Lygonia between Puritan sympathizers and royalists. The way was open for a takeover. In every case, though not without occasional prolonged resistance, the Massachusetts commissioners secured a written capitulation to the authority of the Bay Colony, which replaced with a vigorous, effective government the feeble attempts at absentee rule by feudal proprietors.

With the Restoration of the Stuart monarchy in 1660, the crown, urged on by heirs with interests in Maine and New Hampshire, tried to strip Massachusetts of her northeastern possessions as part of a general program to curb and discipline an obstreperous colony that had far overstepped her bounds. At length, following a period of confusion, the general court simply bought the title to Maine from the heir of Sir Ferdinando Gorges. There was a time of virtual anarchy again in the 1680s, when the original Massachusetts charter was lost and Sir Edmund Andros governed the short-lived Dominion of New England, but the new provincial charter of 1691 once more made Maine, along with the old Plymouth colony, part of Massachusetts. So it remained until the Missouri Compromise.

But from the Massachusetts point of view, this was by no means enough. Maine must be absorbed into Massachusetts in every possible way, not simply owned by it. And so religious imperialism followed political imperialism, and this is where Cotton Mather's desert imagery came in. The work of evangelizing the Maine settlements that had recently been brought within Massachusetts was carried on not by Mather, who stayed mostly in Boston, but by a handful of hardy young parsons a few years younger than he. They had grown up on the Massachusetts North Shore and gone to Harvard during the rectorship of Increase Mather, Cotton's father.

Maine had seen ministers before, but they had come sporadically and their visits had usually been brief, controversial, and generally ineffective. There had been notable exceptions, especially Shubael Dummer, who was killed at York in 1692 in one of the bloodiest massacres of King William's War after he had served the first permanent church in Maine about twenty years. There had also been John Brock, who ministered heroically to the turbulent fishing community at the Isles of Shoals in the 1650s and early 1660s. But by the time King William's War was half over, the religious scene in Maine was as desolate as Cotton Mather claimed it was, and it was almost as though it had never been otherwise.

As if in response to the terrible state of affairs that the war had brought to the Bay Colony's new eastern possession, and in answer to Mather's lament, a tiny army of missionaries suddenly appeared in frontier garrisons and nearly abandoned towns. There these devoted emissaries of the religion and culture of Boston and Harvard spent the rest of their lives. John Newmarch went to Kittery, and John Wade first to some military garrisons in the vicinity of Brunswick and then to Berwick. Samuel Emery served as military chaplain at Wells and then as settled minister there. Samuel Moody went to York as chaplain and then began an almost legendary forty-seven-year pastorate in the same place. Jeremiah Wise ministered to a military garrison at Saco and then moved to Berwick, where he succeeded Wade, who died in 1703. All these young men had been born within seven years of one another in either Ipswich or Newbury, Massachusetts. They had all arrived in Maine in their early twenties. Several other contemporaries of theirs from the same vicinity took up pastorates in established churches in southern New Hampshire at about the same time. An older man, John Pike, minister of Dover, spent part of an eleven-year absence from his parish during the war as chaplain to the extreme frontier garrison at Pemaquid.

This was a remarkable fraternity, obviously motivated not by profit or social standing but rather by some common perception, a "group mind" perhaps, that gave every member a similar vision and a similar mission to carry out in a dangerous and then singularly unattractive wilderness. None of these men articulated such a vision or mission, at least in any way that has come down to us, but that is not surprising. None was at the top of his Harvard class, none showed any special precocity as a youth, and none left much in the way of published writings, except for a few printed sermons by Samuel Moody. All were practical men, moderate in theology, devoted to the material and moral welfare of their communities. They were shirt sleeve parsons, at least in a figurative sense, not given to elaborate theorizing or perhaps even to original thought. But they were a dedicated and exceptionally effective group, responsible in large measure for civilizing and regularizing community life along the Maine coast as far as Casco Bay between 1700 and about 1750. The vision to which they responded and the mission to which they gave their lives must have been very close to the one that was best articulated by Cotton Mather.

New England, an episode in Christian history even more than a place on the map, was being and would continue to be challenged and judged. Her trials were at once a judgment, a punishment for apostasy, that demanded repentance and a reformation of morals, and a temptation, a challenge to steadfastness in the faith and to a continuation of the commitment to the original mission. During King William's War, both the judgment and the challenge were focused on the eastern frontier, a barren wasteland that must be watered by the spirit of the Puritan God and where the terrible trials of the Tempter must be encountered and overcome. In these ways, the original mission of New England would be vindicated, and the church militant advance toward the final victory of the church triumphant. It was with such a vision and such a mission that this hardy little army of young missionaries invaded the desert.

Cotton Mather had been right in 1698 when he guessed that

the abandoned parts of Maine would be settled again. More-over, there were vacant lands just inland from the tier of coastal settlements that pioneers could reach with relative ease. But there was still another war to endure before the inevitable expansion of settlement could proceed with acceptable safety. The year following the end of King William's War in 1689, the Massachusetts General Court set up a seven-man Committee on Eastern Claims to examine all titles and claims to land in the deserted areas. The idea was to guarantee that the resettlement would be as free as possible from land controversies, but the committee had scarcely begun its work when a chain of events in Europe precipitated the War of the Spanish Succession in 1702. These events led to renewed hostilities between enemies (the English versus the French and Spanish) that were now becoming traditional in America, where the conflict was known as Queen Anne's War. There followed another eleven years of fighting and destruction just as horrible as the other. Maine again was left in ruins.

During the quarter-century before 1713, when the Treaty of Utrecht brought the wars of Louis XIV to a close and instituted a European peace that would last for twenty-seven years, the expansion of settlement in the northern colonies in America was all but impossible. Nevertheless, the population of eastern Massachusetts and southern New Hampshire continued to grow by natural increase, towns became more densely settled, and another generation grew to maturity and wanted farms. When the artificial constraints of frontier warfare ended, therefore, the urge to break out into new territory was sudden and dramatic. At the same time that the wars had prevented geographic expansion, they had helped create capital among the merchants of Boston and Portsmouth who had profited from wartime trade. Since the Restoration, England had experienced speculative fever; now, with new American capital available as well, the fever reached the colonies.

The purchase of the Plymouth colony's Kennebec lands by some Boston merchants back in 1661 had provided an early glimpse of the future, at a time when the English speculative boom had barely begun. The purchasers had known that the fur

trade was dwindling—that, indeed, is why Plymouth had sold
out—but in addition to what might be salvaged immediately,
there had been the prospect of selling timber and masts, setting
up shipyards, and eventually selling off farms. This, then, was
speculation—speculation in land, which was a new idea in New
England. As it turned out, the move had been premature; the
purchasers had not counted upon the long chain of Indian hostilities beginning with King Philip's War in 1675, and the consequent abandonment of the eastern frontier for much of the
next fifty years. But their successors, incorporated in 1753 as
"The Proprietors of the Kennebeck Purchase from the late Colony of New Plymouth," were more fortunate. In the eighteenth
century, helped along by various Massachusetts enabling acts,
companies such as this one, and also the Lincolnshire Company, the Sheepscott Proprietors, the Pejepscot Proprietors, the
Wiscasset Company, and the Pemaquid Proprietors, became the
instruments for the sale, settlement, and incorporation into
towns of most of the land between Casco Bay and Pemaquid. A
new form of Massachusetts imperialism in Maine was born.

And although the wars with the French and Indians were over
for the time being after 1713, and families could safely resettle
abandoned townships or move into the vacant near interior to
establish new communities, the Massachusetts authorities would
be concerned with defense as long as Canada stayed in French
hands. One way to assure the safety of Boston was to have a
well-settled frontier far enough away to engage an attacking
force well before it could do any damage to the more populated
areas. Cotton Mather had a phrase for it in the title of an essay
he published in 1707, *Frontiers Well-Defended*. Therefore, the
general court granted a dozen or so six-mile-square townships to
various groups of proprietors to fill in the vacant inland territory
between the northern points of Falmouth (modern Portland) and
Berwick, across the Salmon Falls River from New Hampshire.

Despite the urge to move to new land, despite the speculative
fever, and despite the official encouragement to create new pioneer communities out of a concern for defense, the actual peo-
pling of the Maine frontier in the years between 1713 and the
outbreak of King George's War in 1740 lagged behind expecta-

tions. It was not easy to survey a township, clear five to ten acres per family for crops, build little log houses, lay out roads, find someone willing to risk the expense of damming a stream and building a saw- and gristmill, band together as a community to build a meetinghouse, fort, and schoolhouse (or combination), and locate young Harvard men to come to the wilderness to serve as ministers and schoolmasters. The terms of each grant required all of these. Though the terms were seldom met within the prescribed time, no grant was ever rescinded. Eventually, towns such as Windham, Gorham, Standish, Sanford, Lebanon, and Buxton became established in the defensive zone and developed through a slow process from pioneer hamlets into dispersed communities of family farms, a new kind of New England town. This was not exactly what the Massachusetts lawmakers, or ministers like Cotton Mather, had in mind. But for those who were able to survive the rough pioneering stage and make it through to the status of country farmer, the result was happy enough, especially since few of the new settlers had shared Mather's vision to begin with. It was also good, in the long run, for Maine.

Meanwhile, the proprietors of the various land companies that held tracts east of North Yarmouth, a formerly abandoned Casco Bay township that was resettled by an elaborate process overseen in every detail by a committee appointed by the general court, began to realize some of their speculative ambitions. The Pejepscot Proprietors, for example, laid out the towns of Brunswick and Topsham and shipped settlers and their goods from Massachusetts at no charge. The Sheepscot Proprietors, who owned land further east, operated in a similar way. By about 1740, the year Samuel Waldo of the Lincolnshire Company persuaded more than fifty oppressed German families to come and farm his land and manufacture iron and lime at Broad Bay, some of these eastern towns were ready for incorporation.

The years between Queen Anne's War and King George's War, then, were years of growth and new development for Maine. In almost every way, it was a growth and development spurred by the men and institutions—province government, ecclesiastical system, or land companies—of Massachusetts Bay.

At one point in this otherwise peaceful period, the eastward expansion of the sprawling Massachusetts octopus worried the easternmost Abnakis and the Jesuit missionaries who still ministered to them so that the Indians renewed open conflict. Late in 1722, there were raids on the new Maine settlements at Brunswick, Arrowsick, and Merrymeeting Bay. By far the most vigorous French missionary in the vicinity was Father Sebastian Rale, who tended a devoted flock of Norridgewocks farther up the Kennebec. Father Rale was suspected, not without reason, of inciting these raids and others, in the same way the English settlers were suspected, with equal good reason, of encroaching unjustly on Indian lands. The Massachusetts government subsequently declared war on the "eastern Indians." In the three-year conflict that followed, a New England force devastated the village of Norridgewock and killed Rale in 1724. In the same conflict, the Pequawkets, a staunch and extremely valiant band of inland raiders, met their last defeat at the hands of an equally valiant company of New England men under John Lovewell of Dunstable during a bloody and lastingly famous battle in Fryeburg on the upper Saco. Soon after that fight in 1725, the brief period of renewed warfare ended, and the work of planting the eastern "desert" resumed once more.

Cotton Mather did acknowledge that this barren, God-forsaken landscape occasionally bloomed in spite of itself. His favorite example was Sir William Phips, hero of King William's War and first royal governor of Massachusetts.

In 1651, while the men of Massachusetts were plotting the absorption of Maine, the wife of an obscure gunsmith in what is now the town of Woolwich on the Kennebec (Mather called it "a despicable Plantation") gave birth to the future first royal governor of Massachusetts and the first American-born British subject to receive knighthood. William Phips, one of twenty-six children, left home at the age of eighteen to apprentice to a shipwright in nearby Arrowsick. Four years later he went to Boston, determined to be a ship's captain one day. There he learned to read and write, married well, and became associated with some Boston businessmen. He made his fortune and was knighted by the king in 1687 after successfully completing the unlikely exploit of raising a treasure worth £300,000 from a long-sunken Spanish ship off Haiti (after quelling a mutiny, incidentally) and returning the treasure to England. He worked with Increase Mather to achieve governmental changes during the tenure of Sir Edmund Andros as governor of the Dominion of New England and, after the Glorious Revolution of 1688, also worked for the restoration of the Massachusetts charter. Under the new provincial charter, Phips served as first royal governor after leading a successful expedition against Port Royal in Nova Scotia during King William's War and an unsuccessful one against Quebec that was designed to reduce all of Canada.

As a member of North Church, of which both Mathers were pastors, the governor supported taxation for the support of Massachusetts Congregationalism and appointed the courts that examined into the witchcraft scare in and around Salem in 1692. Finally, after a brief period of hysteria and confusion, and the conviction and execution of twenty accused witches on no more than "spectral" evidence, Phips suddenly ordered the end of the prosecutions and pardoned several of the condemned witches. Though lauded without reservation in Cotton Mather's *Magnalia,* Sir William's administration did not go unquestioned. He died in England in 1694 while waiting to answer charges of maladministration. With the death of this self-made and graceless but extraordinarily accomplished native down-easterner, the Mathers lost a powerful friend and ally in their fight to restore the old power structure in Massachusetts.

Cotton Mather paid him as high a compliment as a governor could receive. "Though by the providence of God I have been with him at home and abroad, near at home, and afar off, by land and by sea," Mather wrote at the end of the long biographical sketch in *Magnalia,* "I never saw him do any evil action, or heard him speak any thing unbecoming a christian." [6] Not bad for a product of the desert.

But for one who viewed Maine and the world as Cotton Mather did, Sir William Phips was a prodigy, the exception that

6. *Magnalia,* 1:206.

proved the rule. By and large, Maine was a singularly unchristian place, at least in Mather's terms. The moral landscape,
therefore, was desolate, needing for redemption the planting and
the watering that could come only from Massachusetts. Mather
could easily forgive, and even applaud, the fact that it had taken
a conquest to do it.

4

Independence Twice, and
James Sullivan's Romance

FOR all the image-makers from Capt. John Smith to the Reverend Cotton Mather, Maine was a kind of frontier. Here an advance guard of civilization confronted the wilderness. Smith saw here an opportunity for the heroic exploitation of the land and fisheries by patriotic Englishmen. Christopher Levett found a commercial frontier. John Josselyn was a collector of wild curiosities and thought he had glimpsed a touch of prehistoric paradise. Mather saw a religious frontier, a desolate wilderness needing to be occupied for its own good by Christians. All looked in at this wild place from outside, measuring, scheming, imagining, and judging by standards brought from England or Massachusetts. Maine had meaning for each of them only to the extent that it could be fitted into a framework erected elsewhere. It was, in short, a frontier.

James Sullivan was different. He wrote of Maine from the inside. Like his friend Jeremy Belknap, who wrote a book on New Hampshire, and his political hero Thomas Jefferson, who wrote one on Virginia, Sullivan wrote of his place after the people who lived there had acquired a sense of identity with it. Sullivan's *History of the District of Maine* describes Maine and its history from the point of view of an insider; it also presents an apology for it and hints that its people are the better for having lived in this special place.

We are taught to think of the eighteenth century as an "Age of Reason," and so it was. But to think completely about this exciting era, it is necessary to add what is often overlooked. For one thing, the Anglo-Americans of the eighteenth century had not rejected that religious faith which "Reason," in the simple view, is supposed to have replaced. For another, they were hardly so disciplined by the rational process that they neglected the feelings and the imagination that are associated with the "Romantic" period, which came later. The age of Sullivan, then—the age of the American Revolution and the early Republic—was among other things an age of romance. And few writers even of the official "Romantic" age offered such a picturesque, imaginative, inspired accounting as Sullivan provided in his history of Maine. That is not to say that this is "good" history. It is not, for example, nearly as careful, thorough, well-balanced, or scholarly as Belknap's *History of New Hampshire,* which probably inspired Sullivan to write it. Nor does it stand up as well as literature. But for an un-self-conscious expression of the romantic nationalism of the period, one can do no better than read Sullivan.

Sullivan no doubt would have denied it, but he looked at Maine with the eyes of a poet. That seems unlikely enough in view of his biography. He was a lawyer and politician, educated first at home by his schoolmaster father in Somersworth, New Hampshire, and Berwick, Maine, and then in the Durham, New Hampshire, law office of his brother John Sullivan, the revolutionary general. His main competence as a lawyer was in the distinctly unpoetic field of land titles, about which he wrote a book. Before he entered public life, he supplemented his country lawyer's income in Biddeford by selling goods for John Hancock of Boston, one of the richest merchants in America. Through Hancock's friendship and patronage, he got into Massachusetts politics. During the War for Independence he was a justice of the Massachusetts Supreme Court and a member of the legislature. After the war he served in the Articles of Confederation Congress and later as a probate judge. He served

seventeen years as attorney general of Massachusetts and finally, after four unsuccessful tries, was elected governor in
1807. He was re-elected just before he died in office in 1809.

Sullivan's *Maine,* his most lasting monument, came out in
1795, midway between the outbreak of the War for Independence and the end of the War of 1812. The core of Sullivan's
statement is a poetic view of the relationship between natural
environment and human character and of the inevitability of
human "progress." It is also an expression of the new American nationalism and of the local chauvinism with which Sullivan
regarded his "district" of Maine. In all these matters, Sullivan
provides yet another image of the place, an image that reflects
the romantic character of the era of independence.

The *History of the District of Maine,* like Jefferson's *Notes
on Virginia* and the third volume of Belknap's *New Hampshire,*
begins with a precise description of location and borders. In
good scientific fashion appropriate to the late eighteenth century, the author goes on to discuss the seasons and the climate,
but pauses as early as the fourth and fifth pages of the text to
point out the advantages of Maine's cold weather. The winters
may seem "tedious," he admits, but it is far better to endure
"our northern snow banks" than the "fever and ague, and the
other disorders" that plague the southern population.[1] Maine
has a larger birth rate than Massachusetts proper, and infant
mortality is lower—proof that the Maine climate is even better
for human life than that of nearby Massachusetts.

Not only is the northern climate better than the southern for
human life and health, but there are advantages here also in the
lack of precious metals and abundance of fish, harbors, timber,
and arable land. Sullivan's thoughts on this topic remind us of
Smith's: "The expectations founded on the advantages of mines
of gold and silver ore have never failed to produce idleness,
profligacy, and dissipation of manners; while commerce, agriculture, and the fisheries necessarily urge people to industry,
frugality, prudence, and economy: and have a direct tendency to

1. James Sullivan, *The History of the District of Maine* (Boston, 1795; reprint ed.,
Augusta, Me.: Maine State Museum, 1970), p. 8.

render man an active, virtuous and respectable creature.'' [2] He concludes a long essay reflecting upon the bane of "ease and leisure" with this forthright pronouncement: "We may conclude, that the advantages of the northern part of the continent, exciting to industry and toil, are much superior to those in the south, where wealth is expected, without the toil and labour of the proprietor.'' [3]

In a chapter on the Indians, Sullivan paints a fairly savage picture of the Abnakis. One guesses he wished he could have been more complimentary, since one of his consistent purposes is to show the natural advantages of the northeastern environment, which he is convinced affects human character for the better. On the other hand, it is also necessary for his argument to portray the Indian stage as flawed and temporary. He is at least able to conclude that North America compares favorably with Central and South America in its Indians: "On the whole we are obliged to conclude, that the Savages of North America, are, and always have been, more humane and less cruel than those of the South; or that the Spanish writers, in order to excuse the unexampled cruelties of their nation, have deceived the world with tales which had no foundation.'' [4]

Sullivan reveals his strongest powers of imaginative argument in two chapters on his specialty, land titles. One chapter deals with titles to American soil from European governments, none of which he concludes is valid, considered in light either of natural or of international law. Nor, he argues in the next chapter, is there any legal validity in titles granted by Indians. Nonetheless, the white man's possession of former Indian hunting grounds is both fair and legal.

The argument is a long one, resting on a concept of nature and inevitable human progress that stands in a straight line between the natural law of John Locke, the part about property, and the "manifest destiny" of the nineteenth century. The Indians, it is true, had legally used the land in their own "sav-

2. Sullivan, *Maine*, p. 60.
3. Sullivan, *Maine*, p. 61.
4. Sullivan, *Maine*, p. 107.

age" way, but not efficiently and not with any idea of "a permanent use and improvement of the soil." The Indian has now, Sullivan thinks, "had his day." The necessities of human population now make it necessary to improve the land rather than simply hunt from it, which leaves it no more productive than it was before. Therefore, the new occupiers have the same right of occupancy as the old ones once had. Sullivan's argument and his flights of fanciful language show how closely he is related to his romantic successors who justified the conquest of the West. He wrote:

> The earth was made for man. . . . The exigencies of his nature compel him, by toil, to till the earth for food, and the faculties of his mind, prompting him to an excellency in the art, give a certain indication, that he was intended to beautify with dress, and to ornament with architecture, that part of creation which was assigned to him.

There is to be a "progressive improvement" of the world, says Sullivan, until "The mighty mountains, and the deep and dangerous morasses . . . in their turn become subject to the hand of agriculture, and yield to man a compensation for his labour." The world began as "a rude mass of matter"; it will advance finally to "the highest state of elegance to which the noblest refinement of human reason can bring it." There is a progression from "chaos" to "an uninhabited and desolate desert." Then it becomes "the habitation of beasts, and birds; then the haunts of roaming and unsocial barbarians: then the dwelling of savage tribes; and finally the high cultivated, and beautifully decorated soil of civilized nations." [5]

There is no idea of restraint in Sullivan's vision of man's triumph over nature, any more than there was throughout the nineteenth century. Earth is man's; the more "improvement" he can bring to it, the better humanity will be and the closer the earth will come to fulfilling the purpose for which God made it and gave it to man to conquer. The implications of Judge Sulli-

5. Sullivan, *Maine,* pp. 129–131, 135, 139.

van's romantic notions of "progress" were—and are—profound indeed.

His vision, unfamiliar though a "romantic" view of the era of independence may be, was out of character neither with the works of his contemporary historians and natural philosophers nor with the events in Maine that surrounded Sullivan's life and book. Between 1775 and 1815, Americans fought twice for independence, once from 1775 to 1781 and again from 1812 to 1815. Maine was a theater for minor but dramatic episodes both times. These events were full of heroism, valor, and chivalry, or at least so it seemed to contemporary observers, the kind of thing that modern technology and attitudes have made obsolete in thinking about war. Moreover, there was at work a psychology of progress, of human betterment. These struggles against Britain, the first for legal independence and the second for practical independence, were to some extent the ritual shedding of a worn-out European garment that no longer fit and was in the way—a necessary act of freedom on the road toward the fulfillment of the American destiny. It did not matter that nobody ever quite spelled out what that destiny was, or at what point it would be fulfilled. This was a matter of faith, not of logic. But it was not a blind faith, for the signs were there for all to see. Some of the signs were glorious and picturesque; it was, in fact, an age that began with knights and ended with heroes.

For the men and women of Maine, the first glimpse of the future came in a burst of glory and disillusionment in 1745. With the strange success in 1687 of William Phips of Woolwich, Maine had already acquired a knight. In William Pepperrell of Kittery Point, Maine now added another honor, a baronet. Pepperrell was so honored for commanding the ragged army of New England soldiers who captured the French fortress of Louisbourg in 1745. This exploit, even unlikelier than that of the first Sir William, who had raised a Spanish treasure, gave a marvelous boost to English fortunes during the War of the Austrian Succession (King George's War in America) but for Maine especially, it marked the beginning of the end of the English connection.

In 1744, the long-anticipated renewal of hostilities between

Britain and France provided the occasion on each side to try again to conquer the other's American empire. Britain had gained Nova Scotia in 1713, but not Cape Breton Island. The British had gotten much the better of the Treaty of Utrecht; the agreement that the French should have Cape Breton Island, or Isle Royale as they named it, was a concession. It recognized that France needed some protection for the only entrance to her sprawling inland possessions, the gulf and river of Saint Lawrence. With British-held Nova Scotia to the southwest and British-held Newfoundland across the entrance to the gulf on the northeast, Cape Breton was a lonely French outpost, in fact the only remaining French possession on the Atlantic Coast of North America. The treaty had given France the right to fortify the island, and so for twenty years, at a cost of twenty million dollars, French soldiers labored to build a magnificent fortified village overlooking a protected harbor between Gabarus Bay on the south and the tip of Cape Breton itself on the north. The great wall of Louisbourg enclosed an area of fifty-seven acres. The governor's apartments, chapel, officers' quarters, and barracks were all contained in a lovely 360-foot-long fortified building called the Chateau Saint Louis. A large hospital, a bakery, a laundry, a school and convent, a coalyard, many shops, and a village of about a thousand French residents all stood within the wall. A garrison of 700 soldiers manned the bastions, also armed with 116 cannon and mortars.

New England had regarded the building of the fort at Louisbourg with interest and concern since construction had begun in 1720. Through all the years of peace, the harbor there served as a base for the French-American fishery, and as the main port of Canada. Even more obvious to the northern English colonies, however, was the potential threat that this fortified naval base posed to the commerce and seaward defenses of Nova Scotia and New England and the key position it occupied in any plan to invade Canada by way of the Saint Lawrence.

Now that war had begun again, Louisbourg Harbor became a base for privateers who easily preyed upon Maine and North Shore fishermen working the banks of Sable Island and Canso. Eventually, a few of the more daring ones ventured within Massachusetts Bay itself; New England trade came almost to a standstill. The threat ended after a few months when New England merchants fitted out privateers of their own to attack French shipping. For his part, Gov. William Shirley of Massachusetts, having pursued a well-timed military policy that had just led to the successful defense of the British outpost of Annapolis Royal in Nova Scotia, decided in December 1744 that the next step ought to be the reduction of Louisbourg. By a one-vote margin on January 26, 1745, this audacious scheme gained the approval of the general court. William Pepperrell of Kittery, president of the governor's council and colonel of all the Massachusetts militia in Maine, was appointed commander of the expedition.

The story of the Louisbourg campaign has often been told— the crusading spirit, the rush to enlist, the awkward enthusiasm of the New England troops, their unorthodox surprise tactics, the support of the British naval squadron, the abandonment of the main French battery, the forty-six-day cannonading, the surrender terms, the triumphal entry, the Protestantizing of the chapel, the celebrations and the prayers and the sermons throughout New England. William Pepperrell, an instant hero, was created baronet. But in addition, Commodore Sir Peter Warren, the British naval commander, was promoted to admiral, and it seemed to the Americans that an astonished England, almost as if to explain the incredible victory, was giving Warren and the Royal Navy more than their share of the credit.

Then came the most crushing blow of all. By the Treaty of Aix-la-Chapelle in 1748, after the weary army had suffered far more misery and death from boredom and disease during the long occupation of Louisbourg than during the exciting siege, and after three years of renewed border warfare that touched every settlement in Maine, Louisbourg was returned to the French. Never again would New Englanders, especially in Maine, which with its tiny population had furnished a full third of the 3,250 Massachusetts soldiers who composed the bulk of Pepperrell's army, regard their king and their English cousins exactly as they had before. They had been betrayed.

Just how sharply the sense of betrayal cut into the sensibilities of Maine folk is revealed by the extraordinary recollections of a correspondent of mine who was growing up on the Maine coast early in our own century. Mrs. Edna Wardwell Clements, now of Belmont, New Hampshire, spent her childhood on the shore of Penobscot Bay, where many generations of Wardwells had lived since the eighteenth century. Her grandfather had fought in a Maine regiment in the Civil War. But the military experience that had most shaped his youthful consciousness, and the one that he never tired of relating in his old age, was a hundred years in the past when he was born. It was the Louisbourg expedition, which had claimed the lives of three kinsmen four generations earlier. "At 78," Mrs. Clements wrote to me in June 1975,

> I can still hear my grandfather's voice raised, as it frequently was, against the stupidity of England to give back to France this fortress (that would still shelter the marauding privateers that captured our fishing vessels) only three years after 1,000 New England men had died capturing it. I know every detail of the siege, at least Grandfather's version, and he drummed it into me over a period of years that the seeds of the Revolution were sown then and there, by the Treaty of Aix-la-Chapelle, in a bitterness never to pass in the twenty-seven intervening years.[6]

Possibly Grandfather Wardwell exaggerated his inherited resentments; maybe his family's attitude was not quite typical. One thing, though, is certain: The bitterness that was felt and communicated a century and a half after the event must have reflected something, at least, of that which was still fresh on the coast of Maine at the time of Lexington and Concord, Bunker Hill, and the burning of Falmouth.

But bitter resentment against the English was not the only legacy of Louisbourg. On the positive side, New Englanders had shown, or at least so they thought, that they could conceive, plan, and execute a major military operation on their own. And in Sir William Pepperrell, Bart., of Kittery Point, they had a proven hero and leader. Not only was God on the side of New England, as He had demonstrated magnificently at

6. Edna Wardwell Clements to author, June 27, 1975.

Louisbourg, but the men of New England and especially Maine were sturdy, stout, and crafty, more than able to handle their own affairs and make their own destiny.

Nor were the fishermen and sailors of the coast the only Maine Yankees who had reason to begin resenting the authority of Britain about this time. For since early in the eighteenth century, the settlers and sojourners who set up sawmills in the woods from the Piscataqua to the Saint George had carried on a running battle with the various agents who had tried to enforce the royal timber acts. These laws were aimed primarily at preserving suitable white pines for navy masts. Some surveyors general, like Gov. Benning Wentworth of New Hampshire, who held the office from 1742 to 1767, winked at violations of the law in order to avoid conflict with the woodsmen and to acquire easily sufficient mast trees to make a profit while keeping both American woodcutters and the navy board reasonably happy. Others, however, such as Jonathan Bridger and David Dunbar early in the century and Gov. John Wentworth of New Hampshire after 1767, tried with varying degrees of wisdom and honesty to save every tree for the king that the law prescribed. The result was occasional periods of outright "woodland rebellion," as one careful student of the matter has phrased it, and the slow building of conflicts and resentments that inevitably "drove a wedge between the colonists and the Crown." [7]

Then came the last French war, the fall of Canada to the British as the result of the victories of Wolfe at Quebec in 1759 and a combined British force at Montreal in 1760, and new imperial policies aimed at billing the Americans for part of the expenses of keeping up a vastly expanded empire. Most Mainers, as we have just seen, were far from unprepared in attitude and predisposition for the events that began, more or less, with the Stamp Act and culminated on Lexington Green and at Concord Bridge. Maine's response to the Boston Port Bill and the other "Intolerable Acts" of 1774 was like that of the rest of Massachusetts. Some Maine people even thought of themselves as singled out

7. Joseph J. Malone, *Pine Trees and Politics* (Seattle: University of Washington Press, 1964), pp. 82–123, 143.

for special punishment, regarding the Quebec Act as a deliberate attempt to re-endanger the eastern frontier settlements and the punitive Coercive Acts, though aimed specifically at Boston in response to the Tea Party, a deliberate assault upon Maine's overwhelmingly maritime economy. The town meetings of Falmouth and several other eastern towns phrased high-sounding "resolves," sent messages of solidarity to the oppressed people of Boston, and took part wholeheartedly in the movement to send delegates to the extralegal Massachusetts Provincial Congress.

About the time of Lexington and Concord, two Maine communities experienced nasty episodes of their own. These conflicts were enough to confirm all but the most determinedly loyal residents—and Maine did have her share of sincerely principled Loyalists—in bitter antagonism to the British Crown. Early in 1775, a band of backwoods patriots led by the radical Col. Samuel Thompson of Brunswick came to Falmouth, as Portland was then known, and seized Lt. Henry Mowat of the Royal Navy. Mowat, commanding the armed ship *Canceaux,* had been in Falmouth a month to protect a ship being built by a local Loyalist merchant. Mowat sent a warning that the town would be shelled unless the captive was released. Thompson, much to the relief of the townspeople, let the British officer go. Falmouth would soon hear more from Mowat, but meanwhile there was the Battle of Machias.

Machias lies at the head of Machias Bay near the mouth of the Bay of Fundy, less than twenty miles as the duck flies from Eastport. The winter of 1775 had been an especially hungry one for the sixty families of this remote town. In the spring, therefore, when Capt. Ichabod Jones loaded his two sloops for a voyage to Boston, there was even more reason than usual to hope for a speedy and fruitful return. Jones had lived in Machias only a year. In politics, there now seems little doubt, he was a Tory, though whether that was clear to his townsmen at the time is another matter. In any case, arriving in Boston shortly after the shooting at Lexington and Concord, he had to get permission from Vice Adm. Samuel Graves, commander of the port of Boston and of the Royal Navy's North American squadron, to carry provisions back to Machias. The admiral granted the permission only on condition that Jones would bring back timber and firewood for the British garrison in Boston, then under colonial siege. To guarantee the bargain, and to give Jones some protection, Admiral Graves dispatched the armed schooner *Margaretta* to convoy the sloops to Machias. Once in his home port early in June, and before he brought his cargoes ashore, Jones tried to get the townspeople to acquiesce in the agreement he had made with the admiral. At a town meeting, a majority voted in favor of allowing him to take lumber back to Boston. The town was, after all, desperate for food, and an armed British vessel lay in the harbor. When it came to distributing the provisions, however—at least, according to the earliest account—Jones sold them only to those who had voted in his favor. It was this act of discrimination, apparently, that touched off what has been called, somewhat melodramatically, "the naval Lexington."

Armed with guns, swords, and pitchforks, the aggrieved townsmen, with some help from neighboring settlements, seized one of Jones's sloops, the *Unity*, and went to sea after *Margaretta*. Joining up downriver with a small schooner named *Falmouth Packet*, they forced the crew of *Margaretta* to surrender after an exchange of gunfire and some close fighting that cost a total of five lives, including that of *Margaretta*'s captain. Having captured the British schooner in that memorable encounter of June 12, the Machias men transferred her guns to the *Unity*, which they promptly renamed *Machias Liberty*. The newly armed and rechristened sloop, along with the British schooner *Diligent*, captured in neighboring Buck's Harbor on July 15, became the nucleus of the Massachusetts state navy.

Roughly 140 land miles to the southwestward, the 2,000 citizens of Falmouth spent an uneasy summer in 1775, what with the outbreak of war on both sides of them, their dependence on the sea, and their uncomfortable memories of the unpleasantness in May between Samuel Thompson and Henry Mowat. Not even in their most vivid imaginations, however, could they have been prepared for the horror that Lieutenant Mowat would bring their town on October 18.

Mowat actually had reason to be a little grateful to the townspeople of Falmouth, for it was they who had persuaded Thompson to free his prisoner and had urged the rural militiamen who had converged on the town in May to go home. But the memory of "Thompson's War," as the incident had become known, cannot have been far from Mowat's mind as he conned the *Canceaux* into Falmouth Harbor on the morning of Monday, October 16, at the head of a small flotilla of six sail. Mowat had sailed from Nantasket on October 8 under orders from Vice Admiral Graves to "make the most vigorous Efforts to burn the Towns, and destroy the Shipping in the Harbours" in order to "chastize" certain offending towns northeast of Boston. The admiral's list of nine localities, of which Mowat was to attack "all or . . . as many . . . as you can," included three in Maine: Saco, Falmouth, and of course Machias.[8] Admiral Graves had been painfully aware during the months since open rebellion had broken out in April that the Admiralty in Whitehall had begun to suspect that his was a do-nothing navy. Indeed, though he did not know it yet, orders for his recall had already been signed. His response to hints from Westminster that it was past time for some action was to design a campaign of strategic "pacification," as one perceptive writer has called it, aimed deliberately at those New England seaports that for one reason or another had given the British authorities in Boston some specific grievance.[9]

Why Mowat passed by Cape Ann, Marblehead, Portsmouth, and some of the other places on Admiral Graves's list can be explained by winds, weather, and a judgment by Mowat's gunnery officer that the buildings of Cape Ann, designated as the first target, were too widely scattered for effective naval bombardment. Whether these factors are the only reason that Mowat chose Falmouth as his first and only objective is not easy to say.

8. William Bell Clark and William James Morgan, eds., *Naval Documents of the American Revolution,* 7 vols. to date (Washington: Naval History Division, Department of the Navy, 1965), 2:324–326.

9. Donald A. Yerxa, "The Burning of Falmouth, 1775: A Case Study in Imperial Pacification," *Maine Historical Society Quarterly* 13 (Winter 1975): 119–161.

What is certain is that in the late afternoon of October 17, Mowat sent ashore a warning that he was going to bombard the town. A small Falmouth delegation tried to negotiate but succeeded only in delaying the punishment until the next day. The bombardment began at 9:40 A.M. on the eighteenth and continued for eight hours. The shelling with heated cannon balls and flaming "carcasses" was supplemented at one stage by a landing party, which set fire to some shorefront buildings by hand. When it was over, three-quarters of the town was in ashes.

Miraculously, no one on either side was killed, but the ruin of Falmouth's economy and the terrible privation of about 160 homeless families during the winter and spring caused sympathetic vibrations all up and down the coast. Even the British ministry found the first reports of the incident hard to believe. Far from pounding the Falmouth people and their sympathizers into submission, the Falmouth affair, overlooked or underemphasized in most of the standard accounts of the Revolution, spurred a firmer resistance and a greater resolve toward independence throughout the colonies.

Maine's role in the outbreak of revolutionary hostilities, therefore, was far from inconsiderable. Maine also served as the theater for a few of the side actions of the war and as the scene of an epic escape.

One of the most dramatic episodes of 1775 was the futile march to Quebec begun by 1,100 American soldiers, mostly from New England, under Col. Benedict Arnold. The idea was to supplement another expedition up the Lake Champlain–Saint Lawrence route with a surprise movement through the woods of Maine, forming a great pincer against Quebec. Arnold's diminished and exhausted army, accompanied by female Indian camp followers and assorted wives and dogs, emerged from the forest on the shore of the Saint Lawrence opposite Quebec on November 8 after an excrutiatingly difficult march of about six weeks up the Kennebec and then through the big woods. Not until December 31, however, did the combined force make its assault. Arnold was wounded and Gen. Richard Montgomery, commander of the other American army, fresh from reducing

Montreal, was killed. The British garrison beat back the Americans, killing or taking prisoner several hundred. Arnold kept the town under siege for a few months, but in the summer of 1776 he and the Americans abandoned Canada forever. The plan to drive the British out of Quebec and bring its somewhat sympathetic French and Indian residents into the American rebellion had failed. The dreadful march through the Maine woods had been in vain.

In 1777, the year the course of war turned the corner at Saratoga, Maine men from away down east, with the help of the Passamaquoddy and Saint John's Indians, scored two small victories of their own against the British. In August they repulsed a British naval squadron that tried to occupy Machias because it was the staging area for some proposed American raids on the coast of Nova Scotia across the Bay of Fundy. The raids themselves, which took place after the repulsion of the British, were not noted successes, but they did occupy the attention of some of the Royal Navy that might otherwise have been engaged elsewhere and did result in the capture of an armed merchant ship at Pictou.

These small successes of 1777 were more than balanced by the disastrous American defeat in 1779 in Penobscot Bay. In June a British force sailed from Halifax and occupied and fortified a point at Castine. The plan was to establish a naval base to oppose American privateering in the Gulf of Maine and further incursions into Nova Scotia. At the same time, a base there would help secure a supply of ship timber for the navy yard at Halifax. The Massachusetts General Court and Board of War, therefore, mounted an impressive expedition of about 1,000 militiamen in twenty-four transports. Nineteen armed ships of the Massachusetts state navy, led by the new frigate *Warren,* furnished for the occasion by the Continental Navy, escorted the convoy. Late in July, an amphibious force landed. There was some bloody skirmishing, but for several reasons, including the failure of the fleet to back up the landing properly, the British defense held. A British squadron, arriving in mid-August, drove off the Americans who then were forced to destroy many of their own ships to avoid their capture. For Maine and Massachusetts, the Penobscot expedition cost far too much in lives, money, and morale.

Second-in-command of the Penobscot army was Brig. Gen. Peleg Wadsworth, who later settled in Portland and became the grandfather of Henry Wadsworth Longfellow. A Massachusetts Court of Inquiry, convened to investigate the sorry affair, blamed Commodore Richard Saltonstall, the naval commander, but cited Wadsworth for his "great activity, courage, coolness and prudence." [10] Wadsworth further distinguished himself two years later by a dramatic escape from the fort at Castine that his force had failed to capture.

After the failure at Castine, Wadsworth had become military commander in Maine, where from his headquarters at Thomaston he supervised the defense of the coast and tried to prevent trade with Nova Scotia. In February 1781, after putting up a strenuous fight, he was captured in his home at Thomaston by a British raiding party. Wounded, taken to the fort at Castine, and denied parole, though treated with all the gentlemanly ritual that the rules of eighteenth-century warfare required, Wadsworth conspired with a fellow prisoner to escape. It took the two Americans two weeks to cut through the pine ceiling of their room in the officers' quarters with a gimlet and to lay aside enough of their daily rations to take a supply of food with them. On a stormy June night, they raised themselves through the hole in the ceiling, crawled over the adjoining officers' rooms, lowered themselves by blankets to the courtyard, scaled the wall during a torrential downpour, and by a series of maneuvers reached Thomaston after three days.

It is such a series of peripheral actions and events, small successes and failures, and individual exploits that tells the story of Maine's military role in the revolutionary conflict, the first war for American independence. The same was true of the second war of independence, the War of 1812. In this struggle against Great Britain, as in the first, it was Maine's proximity to Canada and above all her economic and strategic ties to the sea that determined her role in war.

10. William D. Williamson, *The History of the State of Maine*, 2 vols. (Hallowell, Me.: Glazier, Masters & Co., 1832), 2:478.

For Maine, however, the War of 1812 was far more than a series of minor dramatic scenes on a magnificent watery stage. It was the catalyst for a momentous shift in internal politics that soon thereafter brought about separation from Massachusetts. Beneath the heaving surface, where Americans fought British, were many dark fathoms of conflicting interests and seething passions. That the new American Union survived this first serious challenge to national policy is a matter of some remark. For Maine, the internal conflicts generated by the embargo of 1807 and the War of 1812 determined a new political future.

The Embargo Act of 1807, successfully urged by President Jefferson in response to British infringements upon American sovereignty, hurt Maine badly. "By the time the law was re-pealed in March 1809," writes Ronald F. Banks, by far the foremost authority on this period of Maine history, "sixty per-cent of the people of the seacoast towns were unemployed and in the largest town, Portland, where the Embargo was estimated to have produced losses in excess of one million dollars, soup kitchens were set up for needy people." [11] Still, the Democratic-Republican majority in the district held, and loyally backed even the declaration of "Mr. Madison's War" in 1812 in the face of the vigorous fulminations of Caleb Strong, the Federalist governor of Massachusetts. There was, however, plenty of Maine-based opposition to the war, especially from the shipowners and merchants of the seaports, who tended to share the antiadministration politics of the Federalist majority in Massachusetts proper. In addition, politics aside, there arose in eastern Maine a brisk trade in contraband with Canada, war or no war. Many lumbermen, fishermen, and owners of small ves-sels, whatever their official political allegiance, took Governor Strong's adamant refusal to co-operate with national military policy as license to carry on business as usual.

All this smuggling in Maine and elsewhere led Congress in 1813 to pass an embargo act even tighter than Jefferson's em-bargo of 1807. "Madison's embargo," as the new act was

---

11. Ronald F. Banks, *Maine Becomes a State: The Movement to Separate Maine from Massachusetts, 1785–1820* (Middletown, Conn.: Wesleyan University Press for Maine Historical Society, 1970), p. 57.

known, practically outlawed going to sea at all; there was to be no coastal trade, not even any fishing outside harbors. No measure could have been better planned to infuriate a people who could not move except by water, which was virtually the case in eastern Maine. The town meetings of Deer Isle, Belfast, Ellsworth, Gouldsborough, and Castine all denounced President Madison and the central government in strongly worded resolutions reminiscent of the various colonial "resolves" of the 1770s, when the target had been the British ministry. Cyrus King of Saco was elected to Congress in 1813 on a platform of extreme opposition to the national government. "If a simple King of England, by his corrupt servants, chastised New England with whips," he shouted, "the administration here chastised her with scorpions. . . . The states of New England can never be satellites." [12] Massachusetts was on the verge of rebellion, and her counties in Maine seemed for a time to be leading the way.

The turning point, both in the seriousness of the war and in Maine attitudes, came when British forces actually occupied first the islands in Passamaquoddy Bay, then Castine, then Bangor, and finally all of Maine east of the Penobscot River— all in the summer and fall of 1814. Casualties were slight, but that was partly because nobody put up much of a fight. In the Penobscot region, confiscation and destruction of property cost the inhabitants many thousands of dollars and cost the British occupying force goodwill that it might otherwise have had.

Finally outraged that an impasse between an obdurate governor and a weak president had led to foreign occupation of much of their own territory and a real loss of property, a majority of Maine people began to demand proper measures for defense and for the reconquest of the territory already lost. At a special session of the Massachusetts General Court in October, it became plain that the Federalist majority, while willing to grant new borrowing powers to the governor, intended the money to be spent primarily on the defense of Boston; Maine, where the

---

12. Samuel Eliot Morison, "Dissent in the War of 1812" in Morison, Frederick Merk, and Frank Friedel, *Dissent in Three American Wars* (Cambridge, Mass.: Harvard University Press, 1970), p. 11.

enemy really was, was neglected. "No event in all the previous history of the union of Massachusetts and Maine," Ronald Banks has commented, "so blatantly revealed the extent to which the interests of Maine could be sacrificed to those of Massachusetts proper." [13] By December, the reinvigorated Democratic-Republican majority of the district and even some Federalists were discussing secession from Massachusetts. The end of the war made further discussion unnecessary for the moment, but only for the moment. The British occupying force sailed home in April.

So much for politics. The military action in the Maine theater was every bit as picturesque as it had been three decades earlier. The most noted was a famous sea fight, remembered for its drama and its chivalric sequel rather than for its strategic importance.

On the fifth of September 1813, about noon, young Josiah Starling climbed the steep hill that rises sharply from the little harbor to the high point on Monhegan Island, where the lighthouse stands. With him was his father, one of about fifty inhabitants of the island, who made his living from farming and fishing. According to Josiah's recollection decades later, they were joined by three officers from the British brig *Boxer*. They had come ashore the day before for hunting and could not make it back to their ship in time for the approaching action with the American privateer *Enterprise*.

The *Boxer* had been patrolling Maine waters for the whole summer, though the British had been lax in enforcing the blockade here in the quite reasonable hope of encouraging the New England states to stay neutral in the war. Unknown to young Josiah, the British ship had in fact just escorted a Swedish smuggler, the *Margaretta,* laden with British goods from New Brunswick and manned by a Yankee crew, to the mouth of the Kennebeck. The cargo was to be sold to American merchants in Bath. To put up a good appearance, the *Boxer* fired a few guns over the *Margaretta* as she proceeded upriver. Fishermen farther west along the coast heard the token firing and excitedly reported it to Capt. William Burrows of the *Enterprise* in Portland

13. Banks, *Maine Becomes a State,* p. 60.

Harbor. He had been searching for the *Boxer* all along. The two ships were now meeting, the *Enterprise* sailing eastward out of Casco Bay, leaving Cape Small and Seguin Island to port, and the *Boxer* standing out of John's Bay, where she had spent the night.

In his old age, Josiah said he remembered it "''s if 'twaz yesterday. I saw the hull on it—'n' 'twaz a big fight.''

The *Boxer* 'd discovered the brig, 'n' under full sail, steerin' 'bout sou-sou-east, bore daown the bay, but tew late, fer the Yankee shot squar' cross 'er bow, hauled upt' the wind, keepin' t' th' s'uth'ard past M'nhiggin in sarch 'f the *Rattler*, w'ile the Britisher gave starn chase. The *Rattler* [another British ship, now departed from the area, which had been patrolling with the *Boxer*] hed gone.

The Yankee hauled in sail 'n' gut reddy for 't fight. The *Boxer* cum up, 'n' poured in a wild bro'dside, w'en the *Enterprise* whirled short on 'er heel, 'n' just raked the *Boxer* fore 'n' aft. A few minits arter, she passed her starn with a secon' rakin' fire. The *Boxer* wuz completely outsailed. In less than a half-hour, a third rakin' fire wuz sent 'cross the *Boxer*'s bows, thet bro't daown the main-topmast 'n' er numer o' men who wuz tryin' t' tare her flag from whar it had been nailed,—'n' the fight wuz over. The ships wer' side by side, 'n' the smoke hed drifted aout ter sea. 'Twuz jest a wood workin' breeze, 'n' the *Enterprise* sailed raound 'n' raound her enemy, no daoubt disabled the fust fire.[14]

While Josiah Starling and his father watched spellbound through a spyglass from Lighthouse Hill on Monhegan Island, there was another fascinated observer fifty sea miles off to the west. Capt. Lemuel Moody, keeper of the Portland Monument Association's new wooden observation tower atop Munjoy Hill in Portland, kept track of the distant action through the association's powerful French telescope, furnishing a salvo-by-salvo account to the crowd at the base of the tower.

The victorious *Enterprise* brought her prize into Portland Harbor the next day. Forty-six of the *Boxer*'s 104 men, including her captain, had been killed in the battle. The *Enterprise* had lost only a small handful, but one had been Captain Burrows. In an extraordinary public funeral in which the crews of both ships

---

14. As quoted by Ida Sedgwick Proper in *Monhegan, the Cradle of New England* (Portland, Me.: Southworth Press, 1930), p. 238.

marched through the streets to the graves, the two captains were buried side by side in Eastern Cemetery on a Portland hillside.

Henry Wadsworth Longfellow, a certified Romantic, was a lad of six when that crowd clustered about the foot of the Portland Observatory. Forty-two years later, he recalled it this way:

> I remember the sea-fight far away,
>   How it thundered o'er the tide!
> And the dead captains, as they lay
> In their graves, o'erlooking the tranquil bay
>   Where they in battle died.[15]

Heroism, chivalry, romance: themes of the age of Sullivan as much as the age of Longfellow, and no less than reason a part of the mind of the Age of Revolution. There was another theme as well, and that was independence. America fought Britain for it twice, and by the end of the War of 1812, there were many in the district of Maine who were thinking seriously about independence from Massachusetts. James Sullivan, back in 1795, had thought about statehood for Maine as another aspect of the march of "progress" that he considered inevitable. Maine, wrote Sullivan at the end of his history, "is so large and populous, and its situation so peculiar, that it cannot remain long a part of the commonwealth of Massachusetts." Statehood had actually been discussed now and again for about a decade when Sullivan made this confident prediction. He recognized some difficulties with the idea and regretted the pain of disassociation, but looked forward to "that elevated prosperity, and high degree of importance, to which the District must, from its peculiar advantages, be finally raised." [16]

American nationalism, manifest destiny, local chauvinism—all these complex and deep-seated emotions, romantic rather than rational, impassioned rather than reflective, mark Maine's most important literary document of the era of independence. It is important to notice that in none of these concerns of the heart was there any room for gaiety or tomfoolery. Sullivan was dead serious.

15. "My Lost Youth," F. O. Matthiessen, ed., *The Oxford Book of American Verse* (New York: Oxford University Press, 1950), p. 124.

16. Sullivan, *Maine*, p. 396.

5

Maine Comes of Age

*J*AMES SULLIVAN'S earnest, heavy-handed musing of 1795 about the inevitability of human progress and the coming statehood of Maine reflected the state of mind of a people poised between insignificance and self-fulfillment. It was an anxious period for Maine. The urge to define identity and to vindicate one's place took on a stridency that now seems out of character with the relaxed wisdom that we associate with the economical utterances of the most quotable Mainers of our own time.

In January 1830, by contrast, the readers of the new *Portland Daily Courier* were introduced to an amusing caricature of themselves named Maj. Jack Downing. Jack Downing of Downingville, "about three miles from the main road as you go back into the country, and . . . *jest about in the middle of down east,*" [1] was the creation of the *Courier*'s thirty-seven-year-old publisher, Seba Smith, a native of Buckfield and a boyhood resident of Bridgton. Smith's self-taught pioneering childhood, marked by various manual jobs and a stint at teaching school, had led finally to Bowdoin College and an honors degree, some coastwise and transatlantic travel, and the beginning of a newspaper career with the *Eastern Argus,* a Democratic journal in

1. Seba Smith, *The Life and Writings of Major Jack Downing,* 3rd ed. (Boston: Lilly, Wait, Colman, & Holden, 1834), p. 19.

Portland. His *Courier,* begun in 1829, was to be nonpartisan. His main object in creating Jack Downing, a rustic character who made folksy and often hilariously naive observations in Maine dialect on state and national politics, was political satire. It was successful satire, too, getting in wry digs at the confused state of the Maine legislature, politics, war, the leading national public figures of the day, and Jacksonian Democracy. But in addition to creating the prototype for every cracker barrel philosopher and country oracle who has enlivened American journalism and literature ever since, Smith created a *regional* character, the Downeast Yankee. In laughing at his droll creation, Smith's Maine readers were knowingly and uncomplainingly laughing at themselves.

"The comic comes into being," an oft-quoted aphorism has it, "just when society and the individual, freed from the worry of self-preservation, begin to regard themselves as works of art." [2] Jack Downing was such a work of art. And as his readers recognized in him their own biographies, their own provincial attitudes, their own natural wisdom, wit, and language, they realized that they themselves could boast a special character that was attracting notice from places as far away as Smith's Downing letters were being read. Judging from the numerous attempts at imitation in other areas, that was most of the country.

The steps by which Mainers came to achieve such a comfortable view of themselves were many and complicated. But the essential one was statehood, the coming of political maturity, which was both a reflection of and further stimulus to the social and cultural maturity that allowed an easy sense of self. With statehood, Maine came of age as a government. With Jack Downing, Maine came of age as a people.

When James Sullivan predicted in 1795 that Maine would soon be separated from Massachusetts, the movement for state-

---

2. Henri Bergson quoted by Constance Rourke in *American Humor: A Study of the National Character* (New York: Harcourt, Brace & Co., 1931), p. 12, and by Robert Lowell Russell in "The Background of the New England Local Color Movement" (Ph.D. diss., University of North Carolina, 1968), p. 12.

hood was already ten years old. Responding to a suggestion from the *Falmouth Gazette,* Maine's first newspaper, thirty delegates, dominated by what Ronald Banks calls the "more substantial" element or "cocked hat set," met on October 5, 1785, in Falmouth's First Parish meetinghouse to discuss the possibility. This first meeting, despite some vociferous opposition, led to a convention of delegates elected from twenty towns in January 1786. By that time a more moderate leadership had taken over and the convention did no more than approve a list of grievances against the Massachusetts government. News of Shays's Rebellion in western Massachusetts quickly cooled the sentiment for separation in Maine, where merchants and property owners who feared a debtors' uprising or mob rule did not care to add to the problems of a Massachusetts government concerned with maintaining order. As the decade went on, improved economic conditions in the district and preoccupation with the federal Constitutional Convention and the ratification struggle tended to wipe away even the remnants of a movement that had been led in the first instance by prominent figures like Gen. Peleg Wadsworth, who had wanted primarily to have a state that they themselves could govern.

In the spring of 1791, the separation movement was revived. By then, continued postrevolutionary immigration from Massachusetts and New Hampshire into the new townships in the Maine backcountry had raised the population of the district to more than 96,000—an increase of 40,000 since the end of the war. Again, the leadership came principally from a small group of ambitious, well-to-do politicians, but much of its support came from the new settlers in Lincoln County, where the interests of squatters collided with the claims of absentee proprietors in Massachusetts proper. These settlers, however, had small enthusiasm for the leaders of the separation movement, and vice versa. The main opposition came from merchants and shippers in the well-populated seaport towns of York County, where men in business wanted their political capital to remain in relatively nearby Boston rather than move to some more remote part of upland Maine. The vast majority of voters remained indifferent.

In the end, it was indifference rather than opposition that killed the movement a second time.

After 1800, the leadership of the separationists switched from the Federalist old guard to the Democratic-Republicans. In the decade of the 1790s, Maine gained another 55,000 new inhabitants and some vigorous new leaders of Jeffersonian inclinations who proved more than an adequate challenge to the Federalists. Chief among them was William King, prosperous capitalist of Bath, who with his fellow Democratic-Republicans warmly courted the sympathies of the new settlers and sought independence from the economic and political constraints of the Federalist-led government of Massachusetts. King came to dominate both his party and the separation movement.

The turning of the tide came during the War of 1812, when it became obvious that both a Federalist governor and a Federalist-dominated Massachusetts General Court were quite ready to sacrifice the interests of Maine, even during a foreign invasion.

Even so, the victory of the separationists was not immediate. King and his followers undertook strenuous organizing activities in 1815, with the result that the general court agreed to a Maine referendum to be held May 20, 1816, a month after that year's regular spring elections. The Maine voters, dividing roughly but clearly along party and geographical lines—the Democratic-Republican interior against the Federalist seacoast—cast 10,391 votes in favor of separation and 6,501 against. The separationists claimed a clear-cut victory, but only 44 percent of nearly 38,000 eligible voters had participated, as opposed to the nearly 75 percent of Maine's voters, for example, who had voted in the previous month's Massachusetts gubernatorial election. When compared with the total population of the six counties in the district, which by 1816 had reached about 270,000, those who cast ballots in the referendum amounted only to about 6 percent. Confronted with this doubtful mandate, the Federalist-dominated general court authorized a convention to be held in Brunswick in September 1816 to draw up a constitution for the new state, provided Maine voters approve the separation by a majority of "five to four at least" at *another* referendum to be held immediately beforehand. The results of the new referendum were close, 11,969 to 10,347, but the majority of the convention delegates pushed through a resolution affirming that the "five to four" provision had, by some odd construction, been met. The Massachusetts General Court dismissed that contention as the nonsense that it was and dissolved the convention.

The separationist leaders obviously had committed a tactical as well as moral error by their behavior at the Brunswick Convention. The discredit they earned for their tactics was richly deserved, and the issue lay dormant for the next three years while Federalist strength in the district reached its highest point in two decades.

William King, urged on by some of his fellow Jeffersonians, revived the issue of separation in 1819 when it became apparent that neither he nor his party would ever again enjoy substantial influence on the larger stage of Massachusetts. The general court set another referendum for July 26, 1819, requiring a 1,500-vote margin for approval of the question. This time, King and his men had done their work well. All remaining objections had been answered, King had promised to appoint an appropriate proportion of Federalists to state office, and the people of Maine evidently were ready to close the issue at last. The vote for separation was 17,091 to 7,132—exceeding the required margin many times over.

The voters of Maine had now spoken overwhelmingly for statehood. The next job was to frame a constitution, and the next job after that was to secure admission to the Union. The first was done by 274 delegates to a convention held in the First Parish Church of Portland in the autumn of 1819. Not surprisingly, the delegates modeled the constitution on that of Massachusetts, but the departures from it in detail were far from insignificant. In every case, the changes reflected the overwhelming dominance of the convention by democratically inclined lawyers, businessmen, Democratic-Republican politicians and small officeholders, Methodist and Baptist dissenters against the established Congregationalism of Massachusetts, and in general precisely the sorts of people who had migrated into Maine in huge numbers since the close of the War of Independence. The most prominent and obstinate opponents of separation had been conspicuous at Brunswick in 1816 but did not even come to the Portland convention. This was not the first time, nor would it be the last, that the future of Maine would lie in the hands of recent immigrants from Massachusetts.

The Maine Constitution, therefore, established absolute freedom of religion, provided for universal adult manhood suffrage without any property qualification, omitted the property and religious tests that the Massachusetts Constitution imposed on the governorship, provided a mechanism by which Bowdoin College would be granted state funds only if it submitted to a kind of state control, and provided for taxation of unimproved lands held by speculators on the same basis as settled land. The formula apportioning representatives to the house of representatives tended to favor the smaller towns at the expense of the large; during the debate on that issue, someone quoted Thomas Jefferson to the effect that large towns were "sores on the body politic" anyway. And county delegates to the senate were apportioned on the basis of population, not on the basis of the wealth of the counties, as the Massachusetts Constitution provided. All in all, says Ronald Banks, "the Maine Constitution emerges, with the constitutions of several Western states, as one of the more democratic constitutions of the time." [3] In fact, he suggests, "it can be plausibly argued that the separation movement, after it was captured by the Republicans, was a movement to democratize political and economic life in Maine." [4] The voters overwhelmingly approved the proposed constitution, 9,040 to 797, when it was submitted to a referendum on December 6.

Nobody concerned with the quest for Maine statehood guessed that the final hurdle, admission to the Union, would be more than a formality. Unfortunately for the cause, however, it was a victim of wretched timing. Its proponents had not counted

3. Ronald F. Banks, *Maine Becomes a State: The Movement to Separate Maine from Massachusetts, 1785–1820* (Middletown, Conn.: Wesleyan University Press for Maine Historical Society, 1970), p. 154.
4. Banks, *Maine Becomes a State*, p. 207.

upon having to deal with the ugly spectre of sectionalism, much less having to confront a moral choice in the pursuit of their goal. When the Maine bill was introduced in the House and Senate in December 1819, Congress had had before it for many months a bill for the admission of Missouri. Representative James Tallmadge of New York had made slavery a national issue for the first time since the federal convention debates by proposing an amendment to forbid the further introduction of slaves into Missouri and to free at the age of twenty-five all children born to slaves already there. In effect, of course, the Tallmadge amendment would have brought about the gradual elimination of slavery in Missouri. The Tallmadge amendment had passed the House after a month's debate but had lost in the Senate, where the representation was divided almost equally between slave states and free. (The division became exactly even with the admission of Alabama in December.) Southern senators, however, were stunned by the bitterness of the debate and especially by the skill with which some of the northern leadership had been able to muster votes for what was designed as a first step in limiting the expansion of slavery. Never again until the Civil War would questions of territorial expansion or the admission of new states be separated from the question of the spread of slavery. For the southern states, this conjunction of issues translated into a resolve to maintain at least an equal balance in the Senate. It was Maine's bad luck that her application for statehood coincided exactly with this critical turning point in national politics. When the Maine bill was introduced, powerful figures in both houses, including the powerful Speaker of the House, Henry Clay of Kentucky, made it known that they would favor admitting Maine only if an unrestricted Missouri were admitted at the same time. This was bad news for the proponents of Maine statehood. Political and philosophical complications were now introduced into a question that had long been resolved in Maine and Massachusetts on its own merits. Still worse, if Congress failed to act by March 4, 1820, the nine Maine counties, under the terms of the Massachusetts enabling act, would revert to the control of Massachusetts. Barely three months remained before the deadline—a deadline not for secur-

MAINE

A photographer's essay by Georgiana B. Silk

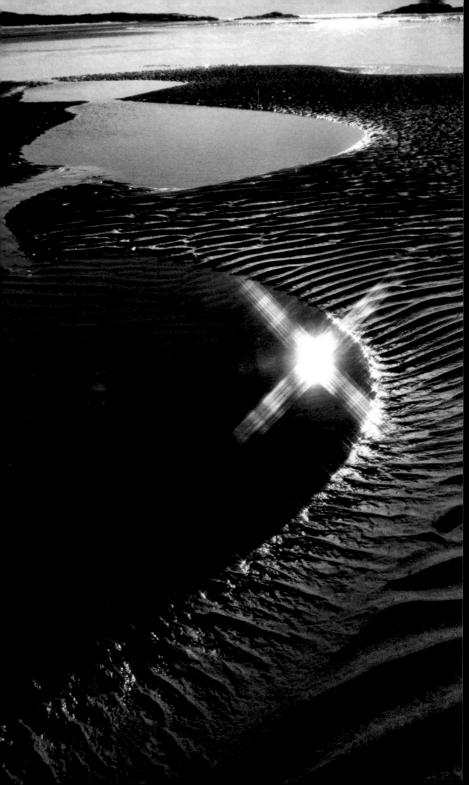

Photographs in sequence

Pemaquid Point Lighthouse Station.
Spruce tree in rocks, Schoodic Point.
Low tide at Popham Beach State Park.
Ferns on Mount Desert Island.
Great Northern Paper Company, Millinocket.
Katahdin Stream waterfall, Baxter State Park.
"Castle Tucker" at Windmill Hill, Wiscasset.
Fishing village of Stonington, Deer Isle.
Stonington lobsterman.
Boy in window, Mount Desert Island.
Deep-draft schooner *Nathaniel Bowditch* in drydock, Stonington.
Lobster pots and buoys in repair shop window, Stonington.
Herring catch, Mount Desert Island.
Derelict ice-haulers *Hasper* and *Luther Little,* Wiscasset.
Western slope of Mount Katahdin.

ing a routine confirmation of what most of the people directly affected clearly wanted, but for unraveling one of the most explosive domestic controversies that the young Republic had yet had to face.

When the Senate Judiciary Committee joined the two measures, many in Maine were outraged. Some of even the most ardent supporters of statehood urged the defeat of the measure, expressing a willingness to sacrifice their dearest cause rather than contribute to the spread of slavery. Portland's two newspapers, the *Portland Gazette* and the *Eastern Argus,* carried on a hot exchange over the matter early in 1820. The two houses of Congress were unable to agree with each other as late as the first of March. Finally, a conference committee of both houses worked out the details of what the history books call the "Missouri Compromise." Both states would be admitted to the Union without restrictions on slavery, but slavery would henceforth be prohibited in the Louisiana Territory north of 36°30′, the southern border of Missouri, with the exception of Missouri. For practical purposes, the compromise meant Missouri would join the Union as a slave state and Maine as a free one. This combination of measures finally cleared both houses on March 3, the day before Maine's deadline. Maine was a state, but the achievement left a bitter taste. Of the seven Congressmen from Maine who were members of the Massachusetts delegation for that fateful session, only John Holmes of Alfred and Mark Langdon Hill of Phippsburg voted for the crucial provision allowing Missouri free reign on the matter of slavery. It passed the House by only 90 votes to 87. Congressman Holmes not only supported the compromise, but was influential in bringing about the conference that made it possible.

Despite ambivalence over the victory, Maine voters quickly forgot their differences over the Missouri Compromise. They celebrated their statehood sumptuously and in the election of 1820 returned both Hill and three of the four dissenters on the Missouri question to Congress. In the same year, the new state legislature sent Holmes to the Senate.

While Maine celebrated and forgot its differences over the issue, however, there were other voices, ominous, barely heard whispers from two former giants of independence, two of the greatest founders of the Republic. John Adams of Massachusetts, very much aware in his eighty-fourth year of the movement for Maine statehood, had written in 1819 that he knew what would happen ''when there arises in Maine a bold, daring, ardent genius with talents capable of inspiring the people with his own enthusiasm and ambition. He will tear off Maine from Massachusetts and leave her in a state below mediocrity in the union.'' [5] Thomas Jefferson of Virginia, eight years younger than his old colleague and sometime political enemy, responded to the Missouri Compromise after John Holmes sent him a copy of his statement explaining his vote on Missouri. Pondering the implications of the sectional divisions that the Missouri question had revealed, Jefferson wrote to Holmes, ''this momentous question, like a firebell in the night, awakened and filled me with terror. I considered it at once as the knell of the Union.'' [6] Fortunately for Jefferson, he did not live to see his dreadful prophecy fulfilled.

Maine's first governor, fittingly, was William King, for whom the achievement of statehood was a personal victory. Once in office, he raised the old question of the boundary with New Brunswick. British and American negotiators had never been able to agree on the location of the line specified in the Treaty of Paris, which had ended the War for Independence in 1783. Now that Maine was a state, the new government had a real interest in jurisdiction and land titles in the disputed area. It was another twenty-two years before two of the most eminent statesmen of the age, Daniel Webster and Lord Ashburton, finally drew the line. Even then, the State Department had to do a little arm-twisting to get Maine to agree. In the two decades before that happened, Maine's confrontations with New Brunswick and with the federal government over the boundary issue raised the hackles and fed the spirits of a people testing the waters of a new identity. And these conflicts provided the set-

5. Quoted in Banks, *Maine Becomes a State,* p. 204.
6. Quoted in Banks, *Maine Becomes a State,* pp. 200–201.

ting for some of Seba Smith's dry depictions of Jack Downing, who quickly became a kind of regional folk hero.

What for the government in Washington was just one of several remaining differences with Great Britain, to be settled by diplomacy, was for the testy new state a question of states' rights. When American and British diplomats agreed to appoint the king of the Netherlands as a referee, the Maine governor argued that the state's constitutional rights would be violated because the state had not delegated to the central government the right to dispose of any of her territory. When the Dutch king actually announced his compromise decision in January 1831, the Maine legislature responded that "no decision made by any umpire under any circumstances, if the decision dismembers a State, has, or can have, any constitutional force or obligations upon the State thus dismembered, unless the State adopt and sanction the decision." [7] Nobody put it that way, but this was a version of the doctrine of nullification. Virginia and Kentucky had applied it to the Alien and Sedition Acts in 1798, Vice-President John C. Calhoun was preaching it at that very moment, and North Carolina would try unsuccessfully the following year to apply it to the Tariff of 1832. This was not exactly northern-style politics, but Maine had gotten her dander up and was not going to be pushed around. That was one of the reasons that the United States Senate, as it turned out, rejected the Dutch king's solution.

Since 1818, when lumbermen from the Kennebec region had settled there and begun cutting timber, the center of the border confrontation had been Madawaska, high on the Saint John River at the very top of a modern map of the state. The Maine men and their French-speaking Acadian neighbors had lived together uneasily in disputed territory until the Fourth of July 1827, when John Baker raised a liberty pole and hoisted the American flag. One thing led to another until Baker found himself in a New Brunswick jail. The Maine governor snapped a

7. *Resolves of Maine*, 2:242–246, quoted in Henry S. Burrage, *Maine in the Northeastern Boundary Controversy* (Portland: Printed for the state, 1919), p. 165.

warning to his New Brunswick counterpart and the legislature went so far as to authorize the governor to protect Maine citizens by force if the federal government failed to do its duty. The John Baker incident was only the beginning of a series of angry exchanges and occasional arrests of alleged trespassers on both sides. By the late 1830s, the War Department in Washington, at Maine's urging, was actually planning the defense of the border while further attempts to survey the treaty line and negotiate a settlement failed.

The comic aspects of the fuss that this little new state was stirring up did not escape the droll pen of Seba Smith. One of Jack Downing's highest moments was his appointment by President Andrew Jackson as an army captain with orders to return to Maine and raise a company of volunteers to "set that business right at Madawaska." His fictional report to Jackson dated at Madawaska November 15, 1831, conveys a satirist's view of the readiness of some of the hotter bloods in Maine to do battle—and of Jacksonian politics:

> The prisoners are out and no blood spilt yet. I had prepared to give the British a most terrible battle, if they hadn't let 'em out. . . . I was pesky sorry they let 'em out quite so soon, for I really longed to have a brush with 'em; and how they come to let 'em go I don't know, unless it was because they heard I was coming. . . . If I could only got down there a little sooner and fit such a great battle as you did at New Orleans, my fortune would have been made for this world. I should have stood a good chance then to be President of the United States, one of these days. And that's as high as ever I should want to get.[8]

The boundary dispute reached its melodramatic climax in 1839 when 205 Acadians with forty-five yoke of oxen spent the winter in Maine-claimed territory cutting timber worth an estimated $100,000. An expedition sent by the legislature to arrest the trespassers failed when the Maine land agent, who commanded the impromptu army, was captured himself. Gov. John Fairfield of Maine and the lieutenant governor of New Brunswick exchanged bitter messages and the legislature appropriated

8. Smith, *Life and Writings of Major Jack Downing*, pp. 156, 159–160.

$800,000 to raise a much larger force and to fortify the boundary against invasion. Henry S. Burrage, a historian, has best told what happened next:

> Thus summoned, men hurried toward the border. It was mid-winter, and only woods roads through the forest for lumbering purposes led thither. First came the hardy lumbermen, leaving their axes and their logging camps and hurrying to the support of the land agent's army on the Aroostook. Following them came other volunteers from towns, hamlets and farms, men and boys, armed only with such weapons as could at once be secured, some of them with muskets used by men from Maine on the battle fields of the Revolution and were with Washington at Valley Forge, or with Pepperrell in the capture of Louisburg in 1745. Later, came the one thousand drafted men called out by the governor's order of February 16th. On February 19th, Adjutant General Thompson declared an added draft of ten thousand, three hundred and forty-three officers and men including field and staff officers, and directing them to hold themselves, fully armed and equipped, ready for an immediate call into the service of the state. This louder call was answered by an uprising not unlike that witnessed in all parts of Maine a little more than a score of years later at the opening of the Civil War.[9]

Congress took the part of Maine without hesitation and ordered military preparations, but also backed President Van Buren in his attempt to get an agreement with Britain for a joint administration of the disputed territory pending a final settlement of the boundary. The president ordered Gen. Winfield Scott, the hero of Chippewa and Lundy's Lane and future conqueror of Mexico City, to Augusta. His mission: to achieve "peace with honor." Old Fuss and Feathers proved an effective negotiator. By his efforts, Maine and New Brunswick backed off from what seemed a certain clash and agreed to a temporary arrangement for occupying the territory that ended the "Aroostook War" without bloodshed before it began. The famous Webster-Ashburton Treaty settled the matter once and for all in 1842 with a compromise boundary that violated Maine principles, but a $150,000 cash settlement from the federal gov-

9. Burrage, *Northeastern Boundary Controversy*, pp. 263–264.

ernment helped sweeten the pill, and the state moved on to new concerns.

The fact remains, however, that Maine spirits had run high over the boundary question for two decades. Maine thus began her new independent political identity with an intense, prolonged exercise in self-consciousness—with, indeed, a sense of selfhood *as a state* perhaps unparalleled in the American experience up to that time. There was a cultural side to this new sense of statehood, too, very much parallel to the flurry of cultural nationalism that had accompanied America's emergence from the era of the Revolution. With astonishing smartness, for instance, scholars and benefactors clustered around Portland were able to provide Maine with a state historical society a bare two years after statehood. Even more remarkable was the torrent of good state and local histories that poured off the press between 1829 and 1833. Gerald Morris has aptly referred to this annual succession of books as "the ancient canon of Maine history": Moses Greenleaf's *Survey of the State of Maine* (1829), George Folsom's *History of Saco and Biddeford* (1830), William Willis's *History of Portland* (two volumes, 1831 and 1833), and William Williamson's great *History of the State of Maine* (1832), which immediately made John Sullivan's history obsolete.[10]

At the same time, John Neal, a writer born in Portland of Quaker parents in 1793, began exploring the peculiarities of the Yankee character, with some particular attention to the extreme version found in his native Maine. For two years, beginning on New Year's Day 1828, Neal edited the *Yankee,* a Portland-based literary journal that helped give early encouragement to Nathaniel Hawthorne, Edgar Allan Poe, and Longfellow but which failed, one sympathetic critic believed, because it was located "a thousand miles too far 'down east.' " [11] Before un-

10. Gerald Morris, Foreword to facsimile of 2nd ed. (Portland, 1865) of William Willis, *The History of Portland* (Somersworth, N.H.: New Hampshire Publishing Co. for Maine Historical Society, 1972).

11. James Brooks, quoted in Benjamin Lease, *That Wild Fellow John Neal* (Chicago: University of Chicago Press, 1972), p. 136.

dertaking the *Yankee* experiment, Neal had outraged many
Maine readers by his unflattering and sometimes crude depictions of American characters in some pieces in *Blackwood's Ed-
inburgh Magazine* and in several books published in London. In
one of these, *Brother Jonathan: Or, the New Englander* (1825),
he had tried to sum up the Yankee qualities in a somewhat
comprehensive way, dwelling at length upon the characteristic
of versatility and even the details of the New England backcountry diet. *Brother Jonathan* was an attempt neither to praise
nor to vindicate, but to describe what had now become a recognizable regional type. After the *Yankee* episode and *Rachel
Dyer* (1828), a tragic novel based on the Salem witchcraft hysteria, which was perhaps his best book, Neal wrote *The Down-
Easters,* published as a series of separate sketches in 1830 and
collected in 1833. Here was an attempt, obviously, to turn from
New England to specifically Maine themes, just at the time that
a state consciousness was being manifested in the other ways we
have noticed. It was not very successful, and it employs an out-
rageously Gothic plot of love and revenge, but the assortment of
characters and dialect is an interesting study in the downeast
writer's emerging perception of his own kind.

But the real key to the acquisition of self-confidence—not
only, that is, a recognition of one's identity but being comfortable with it—is the ability to appreciate one's own eccentrici-
ties. This self-awareness came with Smith's *Life and Writings
of Major Jack Downing* (1833), sufficiently popular that it had
the honor of being extensively plagiarized. Here was the fully
developed downeast character, dialect conveyed accurately not
so much by eccentric spellings as by rhythm and tone, a character busy with the affairs of the Downingville militia and the
Maine legislature and finally with service as a federal office-
seeker and personal adviser to Andrew Jackson. Obviously,
there is plenty of good political satire in all of this. But the letters also provide a very funny characterization of a man from
the backwoods who applies the folk wisdom (and ignorance)
and rude behavior of his native habitat to the larger affairs of
state. By the 1830s, Mainers had come a long way from the
eighteenth century in the way they perceived themselves.

One theme during a cruder and more anxious stage of upper New England humor had been the learned professions. Maine had not been far enough developed in the 1790s to have much of any published humor at all. But if one studies the writings of Royall Tyler, for example, and journals like the *Farmer's Museum* of Walpole, New Hampshire, he will find that a frequent butt of the jokes is a doctor, lawyer, or clergyman whose learned pretensions are deflated by the unlettered natural wisdom of a country bumpkin. It is necessary in this humor to deflate, to scorn, to humiliate the outsider in order to assert one's own self-worth. Not so with Seba Smith's Jack Downing. In one episode, dated July 2, 1833, Jack accompanies Andrew Jackson to Harvard, where the president is to be made an honorary Doctor of Laws. The reader is made amusingly aware of some of the problems of Jacksonian legislation, but when he laughs, he laughs not at Harvard or even at doctors, but at Jack himself:

What upon arth a Doctor of Laws was, or why they wanted to make the President one, I couldn' think. So when we come up to go to bed I asked the General about it. And says I, Gineral, what is it they want to do to you out to Cambridge? Why, says he, you know Major Downing, there's a pesky many of them are laws passed by Congress, that are rickety things. Some of 'em have very poor constitutions, and some of 'em haven't no constitutions at all. So that it is necessary to have somebody there to Doctor 'em up a little, and not let 'em go out into the world where they would stan a chance to catch cold and be sick, without they had good constitutions to bear it. You know, says he, I have had to doctor the Laws considerable ever since I've been at Washington, although I wasn't a regular bred Doctor. And I made out so well about it, that these Cambridge folks think I better be made into a regular Doctor at once, and then there'll be no grumbling and disputing about my practice. Says he, Major, what do you think of it? I told him I thought it was an excellent plan; and asked him if he didn't think they would be willing, bein I'd been around in the military business considerable for a year or two past, to make me a Doctor of War.[12]

12. Smith, *Life and Writings of Major Jack Downing,* pp. 228–229.

Part of the Maine self-image that by 1830 was a "work of art" consisted of the adoption and refinement of the image of the society that was held from without. Late in Cotton Mather's day, while that powerful Boston minister was feuding with an impertinent printer named James Franklin over the smallpox inoculation and other issues, Franklin nevertheless had provided a humorous complement to Mather's image of the Maine wasteland in the December 2, 1723, number of his *New-England Courant,* which he edited with the help of his young brother and apprentice Benjamin. The piece dealt with the declining currency of the title "captain" because of its indiscriminate use by owners of coasting sloops and rural militia captains. Because there were more entries into Boston from the Piscataqua than from any other port, the writer obviously had the skippers of Portsmouth, York, and Kittery as much in mind as anybody:

> What a Shame it is, that a Captain should debase his Honourable Shoulders, and defile his Hands, by sweating early and late under the Burden of huge Logs of common Fuel, fit only to be handled by Persons of baser *Bones,* who have no Honour to lose by such mean Performances? . . . If we enquire into the Reason by the intollerable Growth of Captains, it can hardly be accounted for but by considering, that our Coasters and Country Captains give the Title to each other. . . . Captain *Dishwell,* with a Shoulder of Mutton in his Hand, meets Captain *Strainhard,* rolling a Barrel of Beef along the Wharff, and they make no Conscience of giving Title to one another: One cries, *Your Servant, Captain;* and the other answers, *How do you do Captain, I am glad to see your self well, Captain.* It is indeed a common saying, *Once a Captain and always a Captain;* but it does not therefore follow, that because one is a Captain, we must all be Captains.

That was in 1723, and the author a supercilious Bostonian. On reading Jack Downing's letter of January 23, 1832, downeasterners, much in the manner of the rebel troops who adopted the satirical *Yankee Doodle* as their marching song, were chuckling over their hero's pretentious dealings with his fictitious company of Downingville militiamen, then fortifying the border at Madawaska. He was still only the captain of a company, not yet having attained the exalted rank of major. "And besides," he concludes his letter from Augusta, where he was visiting the "Legislater," "I don't know as I ought to go off jest now, for I had a letter yesterday from one of my subalterns down to Mada-waska, that there's some trouble with my company there: some of the Sarjents been breaking orders, &c. and I don't know but I shall have to go down and Court-Martial 'em." And it's signed, "CAPT. JACK DOWNING." [13]

Maine had come of age, politically as a state and psychologically as a self-conscious people. The boundary controversy helped forge a solidarity and an identity that was at first militantly self-assertive. The sudden outpouring of thorough, scholarly state and local histories, and the crude attempts of John Neal to explore the regional character encouraged a more serious, reflective approach to the Maine identity. Finally, with Seba Smith's Jack Downing, Maine readers learned not only to recognize but to laugh at themselves, the last step on the road to social maturity and an easy acceptance of themselves as a fully developed people. Mainers had not only at last discovered their identity; they were enjoying it. There are few states in the Union, old or new, in which this happy fact has ever been as obvious as it is in what its people have since 1820 proudly called the State of Maine.

13. Smith, *Life and Writings of Major Jack Downing*, p. 168.

6

The Great View Ahead

*O*F all the northern quarters of the Union, Maine is that which will increase the fastest.'' So declared *The American Encyclopedia* in 1808, even before statehood, when Maine's population of about 200,000 was still being augmented rapidly by the incredible postrevolutionary immigration from Massachusetts and New Hampshire. The land boom, timber fever, cramped spaces to the south, and plain postwar restlessness were all conspiring to fill up most of Maine's coastal vacant spaces and draw settlers in unprecedented numbers up the great river valleys. As early as a decade or more before statehood, Maine was being singled out as a place with a marvelous destiny, a place clearly of the future. The great view ahead was embellished upon, especially from within Maine, for the next half-century. An era of vision and enthusiasm was underway.

The encyclopedia article completed the statement thus begun, "and the Kennebec will have the greatest share of this increase."[1] This perception is hardly surprising. The Kennebec region had been the main focus of the great speculators and land promoters of the revolutionary era. Now the Kennebec shipbuilding industry, though at the moment being set back temporarily by the embargo, had begun a boom that would last for

1. Quoted in William H. Rowe, *The Maritime History of Maine* (New York: W. W. Norton & Co., 1948), p. 147.

more than a century. William King had already set in motion the
political machinery that in the long run would make Maine a
state and himself her first governor. The financial and commercial underpinning for King's political career was shipbuilding,
and he had begun that, too. At about the same time, the shipbuilding careers of other magnates such as Peleg Tallman, Abiel
Wood, Jr., and Moses Carlton were taking shape, and with them
the rise of the lower Kennebec River as an extraordinarily lively
center of lumbering, commerce, and real estate transactions.
Bath was the economic capital of this region, and shipbuilding
the king.

But shipbuilding and ocean commerce were not all that made
the Kennebec Valley an avenue to the future in 1808. Farther up
the river was centered Maine's lumber industry, though there
were already signs that the Kennebec would soon lose its pre-
eminence in this critical arena to the Penobscot. For four
months of the year, December through March, woodsmen lived
in the forest, cut pine logs, skidded them over the snow by ox
and horse sled, and piled them by the riverbank. When the ice
broke up in the river, sometime between March 21 and April
24, the logs were tumbled into the water to be carried in spec-
tacular confusion on swollen freshets to downstream sawmills
near the seaports. Lumber was the principal Maine export in the
nineteenth century as it had been in the eighteenth, so the great
river valleys connecting forest with sea were the lifelines of
commerce.

Lumbering, shipbuilding, and ocean commerce seemed to
promise future enough in the giddy decade surrounding the
achievement of statehood, but the promise of Maine did not
stop there. Agriculture, never a staple of the Maine economy in
colonial or revolutionary times, was beginning to take on sufficient importance so that by 1820, according to federal census
figures, Maine's population of 298,000 included 55,000
farmers—compared, for example, with 4,000 businessmen and
not quite 8,000 industrial workers in lumber mills, tanneries,
gristmills, craftsmen's shops of various kinds, and the nine
mills that made up Maine's infant textile industry. Scientific
farming, commercial farming, and agricultural schools were still

in the future, and the opening of the Ohio valley had even now begun to attract settlers who otherwise might have stayed to do their farming in Maine. Even so, by 1820 farmers on 31,000 farms had brought 79,000 acres under cultivation, were mowing hay on another 301,000 acres of meadow, and were sending more than 95,000 head of cattle out to graze on 273,000 acres of pastureland.[2]

Spurred by the embargo and the War of 1812, which had closed off the supply of high-quality manufactured fabrics from abroad, New England began to sprout cotton mills and woolen mills. On the one hand, the new interest in textile manufacturing stimulated Maine commerce because more coastwise shipping was needed to fetch raw cotton from Gulf Coast ports to feed New England cotton mills. On the other hand, it also created a brief infatuation with sheep raising between 1810 and about 1830. Some historians have called this phenomenon the "sheep craze"; Clarence Albert Day, the historian of Maine agriculture, preferred "the Merino fever,"[3] so called from the special breed of expensive Spanish sheep that were imported to New England in great numbers to provide the same quality wool that went into the best English broadcloths. Resumption of trade with Britain and the movement of the sheep industry westward soon cured Maine and her neighbors of the Merino fever, but the experiment had added something new to Maine agriculture. Some farmers continued to raise good-sized flocks bearing the aristocratic genes imported from Spain during the heady teens and twenties. Never, however, did sheep match the importance of dairy cattle in Maine.

But agriculture in general was prospering, and the new state government even provided some impetus. From 1823 to 1831 it made annual grants to the Gardiner Lyceum, a pioneer agricultural school, in 1836 it taxed stallions in order to weed out inferior stud horses, and in the same year it tried to encourage, of all things, silk growing. It did not seem funny at the time; five

2. Clarence Albert Day, *A History of Maine Agriculture, 1604–1860,* University of Maine Studies, 2nd series, no. 68 (Orono, 1954), p. 123.

3. Day, *History of Maine Agriculture,* pp. 101 following.

separate farmers in Maine alone had already set out a total of 20,000 mulberry trees.

In every area, it seemed, Maine was looking to the future, and the future seemed bright indeed. In Bangor, which by 1830 became the center of the lumber industry and the capital of the land boom, the mood was downright reckless. *Niles' Weekly Register*, a nationally circulated newspaper printed in Baltimore, reported from Bangor on June 27, 1835:

> Many speculators here are men of small means. But they have a kind of *dare devil* feeling which is decidedly better than money. A man who is not the owner of one hundred dollars, will buy a township and will sell it again within an hour, at a small advance and pocket the profit, merely transferring all the responsibilities from his own shoulders to those of some other person, or persons, better able to bear them. This is the grand secret of "trade and commerce" in this hot bed of speculation and enterprise.
>
> The ten lots of land which were sold yesterday at 11 and 1200 dollars per lot, were purchased for the sum of $2,500 of a Boston gentleman, who took the land for a bad debt. Here is an increase for land! But this is an everyday story in Bangor. [4]

Conditions like these naturally stimulated dreams of the future. Maine was a new state, full of promise and a spirit of audacious enterprise. Both in her relatively raw condition and in her uninhibited view ahead, she had much in common with the new territories just opening up in the Ohio valley, which even then were drawing settlers from Maine and the rest of New England. Several decades later, a governor of Maine was still able to recognize elements of the "frontier." "She reminds me more of the Western States than of the rest of New England in her condition and needs," Gov. Joshua L. Chamberlain told the Maine legislature in 1870, "—a virgin soil, undeveloped powers, vast forests, and vigorous men, but no money. Like them

---

4. *Niles' Weekly Register* 48 (June 27, 1835): 290–291, quoted in Michael J. Sheehy, "John Alfred Poor and International Railroads, the Early Years to 1860" (Master's thesis, University of Maine at Orono, 1974), p. 11. See also Richard G. Wood, *A History of Lumbering in Maine, 1820–1861*, Maine Studies no. 33 (Orono, 1971), p. 78.

she is trying to build railroads, invite immigration and develop her resources." [5]

Build railroads. Here was the key to development, to the realization of Maine's vast potential for a glorious future that would rival any state in New England and almost any in the Union for prosperity, influence, and the good life of the nineteenth century. Such was the vision of John Alfred Poor, born in 1808 in Andover, Maine, where an enormous space age communications station now links continent to continent by satellite. In his day, Poor conceived the scheme of linking Europe to the interior of North America by an integrated sea-rail system in which Maine would be the crucial link and of which Maine would be the chief promoter and beneficiary. In fact, by the year of his death he had expanded his vision to a worldwide transporation network. His view ahead for Maine was the grandest of all.

As a young lawyer practicing in the bustling Bangor of the thirties, Poor trekked to Boston in April 1834 on purpose to watch the first locomotive in New England make its maiden run from Boston to Newton. For one living in a world of self-contained communities, horse-speed movement, water-powered industry, and wind-powered ships, it was an electrifying experience to see that steaming, chugging man-made monster race along a railroad track for the first time. For Poor, "It gave me such a shock that my hair seemed to start from the roots rather than to stand on end; and as I reflected in after years, the locomotive engine grew into a greatness in mind that left all other created things far behind it as marvels and wonders." [6]

Poor's enthusiasm for railroads became almost too tense to bear two years later as he watched the first stretch of track in Maine being laid down between Bangor and nearby Oldtown.

5. Quoted in Edward Chase Kirkland, *Men, Cities, and Transportation: A Study in New England History, 1820–1900*, 2 vols. (Cambridge, Mass.: Harvard University Press, 1948), 1:466.

6. Laura Elizabeth Poor, ed., *The First International Railway and the Colonization of New England; Life and Writings of John Alfred Poor* (New York: G. P. Putnam's Sons, 1892), p. 26.

He devoted more and more of his time in Bangor to studying
every aspect of rail development and the economy and geography of Maine, keeping track of plans that failed. In 1843 he
made public the dream that had been festering in his mind for
almost a decade: to build two great railroads, one from Portland
to Halifax and another from Portland to Montreal.

Maine, in fact, already had a local railroad line. But there
was ample reason in the state to be suspicious of railroads and
all that they implied for the future, for the present line, owned
mainly in Boston, only served to link southeastern Maine with
the expanding commerce of Boston. And it was competing for
freight and passengers with the Maine-owned sailing packets
that had served as the principal downeast link with Boston for
generations, and with the new coastal steamers that had been
making regular runs between Maine ports and Boston since
1835.

But the vision of John Poor was larger than that of most men;
it was inspired beyond rationality. He even talked in confidence
of "a vision, in which I saw the whole line pass before me like
a grand panorama, and in continuation a vast system of railroads
permeating the whole country . . . ; with new cities with a
dense population; with every facility for ocean steamships from
every country; and the coast of Maine lined with cities rivalling
the cities on the coast of the Baltic." [7] Poor was a romantic
prophet of progress in the tradition of James Sullivan, who had
died the year Poor was born.

But there was also much of the hardheaded and practical in
Poor's inspired drive to make Maine great through railroads. He
pursued his dream like a man possessed with a demon, as indeed perhaps he was, but there was a good deal of sense in his
argument and a good deal of skill in his campaign. Others may
have objected to railroads because they helped only Boston. But
it was precisely to *end* Maine's dependence upon Boston that
Poor projected his "first international railway."

Poor believed all public improvements should follow "the
simplest laws of physical geography and commercial advan-

7. Poor, *First International Railway,* pp. 29–30.

tage." [8] Accordingly, he looked first at the geography of his state. Its area was larger than that of the other five New England states combined. Despite the territorial concessions necessitated by the Webster-Ashburton Treaty, to which Maine had just then reluctantly assented, this great state continued to stick up into eastern Canada like a gigantic thumb, separating Quebec and the upper Saint Lawrence on the west from the "lower provinces," or Maritimes, on the east. It was a productive state in its own right, what with its vast forests and logging industry, its developing agriculture, and its natural waterpower sites, but even more important was its strategic placement for commerce. Maine's many fine deepwater ports were almost legendary. Chief among them was Portland, with its short channel into protected waters that were ice-free the year round, but a town known then throughout Maine as the "deserted village," shamefully short of its commercial potential. Moreover, Portland was closer to Europe than either Boston or New York, and therefore a more obvious entrepôt to North America than either.

Finally, in an outburst of rhetoric closer to Sullivan's style than anything else he ever wrote, Poor argued in one memorial to the state legislature that Maine had the ideal *climate* for an extraordinary railroad project. "The capacity of the human frame for labor," he wrote, "is found to be greater in Maine than in Massachusetts or any State, south or west of it. . . . The higher branches of industry, to be carried on with profit, must seek those regions of the earth where physical exertion is a pleasure, and continuous labor invigorates rather than exhausts the human frame." [9]

So much for the "laws of physical geography." As for "commercial advantage," Poor saw that Maine would prosper more by competing with Massachusetts than by remaining a satellite to it. Montreal and Quebec were frozen in during the winter. Why should not Portland become their year-round port by having a railroad built from Portland to Montreal that would undercut the projected Boston-Montreal route up the Connecticut

8. Poor, *First International Railway*, p. 28.
9. Quoted in Kirkland, *Men, Cities, and Transportation*, 1:207.

Valley? Eventually, the Portland-Montreal connection would form the first leg of the standard route from New England into the west. The second project, the Portland-Halifax line, would route all Canadian traffic between the Atlantic ports and the upper Saint Lawrence through Maine instead of around it. The use of Halifax as the western terminus of an "Atlantic ferry," with a rail connection to New York by way of Bangor and Portland, would shorten the traveling time from Liverpool to New York by at least two days and aggrandize Maine at the same time. Here is how he summarized the advantages of the plan in a petition to the Maine legislature in 1850. It is an example of Poor's vision and his rhetoric at their most convincing:

> Maine, from her frontier position and severe climate, has been heretofore regarded as the least favored of all the states in the Union; while it has the power to become the great manufacturing and great ship-owning state of the Confederacy, if not the first in point of commercial importance. Our climate and our geographical position, generally spoken of as our misfortunes, are in fact the great elements of our strength. The increased necessities which our climate imposes upon us, beyond those of a warmer latitude, are far more than compensated by our superior capacity for labor, our greater power of endurance, and our extraordinary fondness for exertion. With a more extended line of sea-coast than any other state in the Union, and more good harbors than all the other states together, Maine will present at some future day, along her bays and rivers, a line of cities surpassing those which are now found upon the shores of the English Channel, or Baltic Sea.
>
> This result will be hastened by attracting into our own state the great streams of European business and travel, where it shall divide into two great channels—one flowing northward to the St. Lawrence valley and the West, the other flowing southward to the great commercial cities of the continent.[10]

For the first part of his scheme, Poor won the backing of the best brains and money in Portland. But against them was arrayed an even more formidable force composed of some of the biggest political and financial guns of Boston. The two interests

---

10. Poor, *First International Railway,* pp. 166–167.

clashed in a desperate struggle for the favor of Montreal. The scales were already tipped toward Boston, which had planned two routes to the Saint Lawrence and enlisted the support of New Hampshire and Vermont, both of which obviously would benefit from a Connecticut Valley route. Canadian financiers and prospective railroad men were on the verge of committing themselves to building the Canadian end of a Boston connection.

John Poor turned the tide almost single-handedly when he confronted the Montreal men after an epic journey through Dixville Notch in a February blizzard in 1845. Spouting facts and figures based on his usual thorough research and imaginative grasp of the future, Poor demonstrated that a rail route to Portland would be a hundred miles shorter than one to Boston, that a Portland-Montreal route would cross more Canadian territory than a Boston-Montreal route, that Portland was a closer port to Europe than Boston, and that Boston was a rival to Montreal, not the potential partner and supporter that Portland was. The Montreal men drew back from their imminent commitment to Boston, and a week later Judge William Pitt Preble of the Maine Supreme Court, Poor's most influential backer, arrived in Montreal with the charter the Maine legislature had just granted the Atlantic & St. Lawrence Railway. That did it. The Montreal men got a Canadian charter for their end of the link, also called the Atlantic & St. Lawrence, and the bargain was closed. To cap their victory over Boston, Poor and his friends closed out any possibility of a Massachusetts tap into their line by adopting a medium guage for their track instead of the narrower standard American gauge. "Provincialism, Maine and Canadian," Edward Kirkland has written, "won the victory." [11]

Construction began at Portland on the Fourth of July 1846. Seven years later, the trains were ready to roll, but the Atlantic & St. Lawrence was already in trouble. Building costs had far exceeded the estimates, and funding from private investors had fallen short of expectation. The company had managed to push construction through to the end with loans from the city of

---

11. Kirkland, *Men, Cities, and Transportation,* 1:210.

Portland and by getting the construction company to agree to take half its payment in stocks and bonds. But the railroad could not operate under such a heavy debt. Three weeks after the opening, the Atlantic & St. Lawrence leased the line for 999 years to the Grand Trunk Railway Company of Canada.

The abrupt shift to Canadian control of the Portland-Montreal line, the first half of John Poor's magnificent dream, scarcely dimmed the enthusiasm of Maine folk at all—certainly not the enthusiasm of John Poor. Poor moved to Portland about the time he scored his coup at Montreal. Besides plunging into the commercial life of Portland, including the presidency of the Portland Gas Light Company and of The Portland Company, which he founded to build locomotives and other heavy machinery, he acquired a newspaper, the *State of Maine*. The paper became the chief vessel of the railroad gospel in Maine. By 1858, a great new steamship, the *Great Eastern*, was under construction in England. Her maiden voyage was scheduled for Portland. In anticipation, the city built a special wharf to accommodate the 692-foot vessel and her 4,000 passengers, and began construction of a marble hotel. The *Great Eastern*, as it turned out, never came to Portland, but the anticipation of this final linkage of England with Canada and the West by way of Portland filled the columns of Poor's *State of Maine* with ecstasy. Here is one poetic example:

> Portland is looking up, and all her spunk
> Is centered in those noble words—'*Grand Trunk:*'
> That iron arm that links Atlantic '*Maine*'
> With Huron's waters in a single chain;
> On whose smooth rail the swift, careering steed
> Shall cross Victoria Bridge, and onward speed,
> Defying time and space,—its journey o'er:
> Shall slake its thirst on the Pacific shore
> While o'er our waters busy steamers ply
> With flags of every hue, in peaceful harmony;
> A neutral port with every flag unfurled
> That floats on merchant ships throughout the word.[12]

12. *State of Maine*, January 5, 1858, quoted in Kirkland, *Men, Cities, and Transportation*, 1: 213–214.

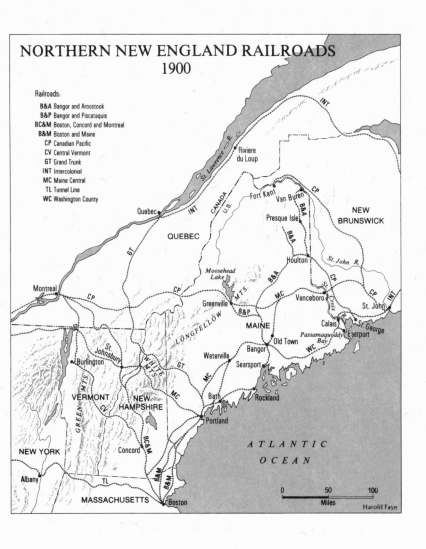

NORTHERN NEW ENGLAND RAILROADS
1900

Railroads:

B&A Bangor and Aroostook
B&P Bangor and Piscataquis
BC&M Boston, Concord and Montreal
B&M Boston and Maine
CP Canadian Pacific
CV Central Vermont
GT Grand Trunk
INT Intercolonial
MC Maine Central
TL Tunnel Line
WC Washington County

Harold Faye

Portland did in fact flourish under the influence of the Grand Trunk. The city's population grew 26½ percent between 1850 and 1860, from less than 21,000 to more than 26,000. Instead of the twenty-fifth largest city in the Union, it became the twenty-third largest. The port became far busier, and though the glamor of the *Great Eastern* fell through, Portland did become the winter terminus, as Poor had anticipated, for the weekly steam packet between Montreal and Liverpool.

Meanwhile, it was time to look eastward. Poor and his friends opened their campaign for the European & North American Railway, which would link Portland and Bangor with the Maritimes and an "Atlantic ferry," with a petition to the Maine legislature in 1850 for a charter and a state-financed survey. It was high time, too, because some Canadian interests were already projecting a line from Montreal to Halifax to be built around the top of Maine entirely in Canadian territory. To sell his plan as a better alternative, Poor summoned railroad men, businessmen, and state and provincial government leaders from both countries to a great convention in Portland in the late summer of 1850. It was a resounding success. Resolutions predicting several kinds of golden ages poured out of the parliamentary machinery with an enthusiasm and unanimity that was almost startling. The proceedings were noted with approval in the press of Canada, Boston, New York, and London. The delegates elected an executive committee to carry on the project. John Poor was chairman. The proceedings in the map- and flag-bedecked Portland City Hall concluded, the convention adjourned after three exhilarating days with "three notable and astounding cheers."[13]

Poor's committee acquired a charter for the European & North American from the Maine legislature, along with the state-financed survey. But various attempts through the fifties to finance the new route failed. Not until the early sixties, right in the middle of the Civil War, did the project get on its feet. This time it was because of a stirring of interest in the thriving city of Bangor, and it was the businessmen and city government there,

13. Poor, *First International Railway,* p. 65.

with encouragement from the state legislature, who got the European & North American going.

Construction of the Bangor–Saint John portion of the European & North American was finished in 1871, but it was a bad job. Poor was dismissed by the other directors early in the game during a quarrel over a construction contract. The superintendent of the job had worked on the new western railroads and applied the hasty pioneering methods of the western frontier here. To complete the pathos, Poor died just fifteen days before the last rail was laid. The financing of the European & North American was just as shaky as that of the Atlantic & St. Lawrence. It was only another eleven years before the line was leased forever to the Maine Central Railroad. Far more tragic for Maine than the financial failure of the company was its failure to bring about the development of northern Maine as it had promised. The Atlantic & St. Lawrence project brought another railroad to Maine, but never fulfilled the promise of Poor's vision.

That failure, however, was hardly the fault of John Poor. Nor was Poor discouraged in the pursuit of his dream by his dismissal from the European & North American. When that happened, he went right to work arousing support for the most ambitious scheme of all, a coast-to-coast railroad wholly within the United States, of which a 1,000-mile Portland to Chicago line would be the key link. From being the port of Canada, Portland, under Poor's expanded vision, would become the port of the Middle West and the Northwest. Through it would flow the traffic of a new shortened round-the-world transportation system of trains and steamships. America would be Europe's passage to Asia, and Portland the port of entry. Portland would also replace New York as the natural shipping point to Europe of the surplus farm produce of the Midwest. "The greatness of Maine," Poor declared in 1869, "cannot be fully comprehended till the Transcontinental Railway is understood, and we realize in practical effect our commanding geographical position." [14]

14. Poor, *First International Railway,* p. 101.

Thus was born still another corporation, the Portland, Rutland, Oswego & Chicago Railway Company, chartered by the Maine legislature. The projected route won the endorsement of the Chicago and Buffalo boards of trade, but not of Portland. The failure of Poor's fellow Portlanders to support his greatest project was the final disappointment with which his life ended on September 5,1871. With Poor gone, the idea simply withered on the vine, and it was left to the Canadian Pacific, heavily subsidized by the dominion government, to complete a transcontinental railroad in the north almost twenty years later. It crossed 145 miles of northern Maine on the way from Montreal to Halifax, part of the way on the tracks of the old European & North American. To serve as a brief right-of-way for a transcanadian railroad was in a sense an ignominious fate for a state that for a moment of ecstatic enthusiasm had pictured itself as owner, manager, and chief beneficiary of a railroad empire of its own. Certainly it was far from the dream of John Poor.

But it was Poor who really got railroads started in Maine, and it was Poor who inspired his fellow Mainers with the most thorough version of the great view ahead. The headiest decades of the vision, and the time that the railroad empire seemed closest to actuality, were the 1840s and 1850s. The same decades marked the climax of Maine shipbuilding, for the years between the discovery of California gold in 1848 and the panic of 1857 were the years of the Maine clipper ships. For a glorious moment, these, too, seemed to be making a fast romantic voyage into the future.

Since the early forties, Maine shipyards had been turning out more vessels yearly than those of any other state in the United States. Donald McKay of Boston led the field in developing the graceful sharp-built ships called clippers, built for speed rather than great cargo-carrying capacity, but Maine builders followed soon. These magnificent vessels proved the backbone of the fleet that carried prospectors, settlers, and supplies 'round the Horn to California. The concentration on Maine-built clippers came in the four years from 1851 to 1854, during which Maine yards launched seventy-seven ships that may properly be called clippers. Fernald and Pettigrew of Kittery built eight of them,

Trufont and Drummond of Bath six, Metcalf and Norris of Damariscotta five, and George Thomas of Rockland four. Thomas's *Red Jacket,* launched at Rockland in November 1853 before a crowd that came from as far away as Philadelphia, could be the most famous ship ever to slip down the ways of a Maine yard. Her maiden voyage in January 1854 set a record for sailing ships between New York and Liverpool that still stands—13 days, 1 hour, and 25 minutes.

But by the mid-fifties, the shipping world began to lose the obsession with speed alone which for a few years had brought the designers and builders of the Atlantic Coast to a peak of grace, beauty, and speed with the magnificent clipper ship. Moreover, by 1857, a serious economic depression undermined the shipbuilding industry altogether. Maine, which in 1855 launched almost 216,000 tons of shipping of all kinds, a third of the total production of the United States, was in serious economic trouble the following year. Shipbuilding declined 80 percent between 1855 and 1859, and between 1855 and 1857, the number of families on relief in the shipbuilding capital of Bath increased from 93 to 220. Not since the embargo of 1807–1809 had Maine suffered so suddenly and disastrously from a blow to her maritime economy. But the clipper ships remained an inspiring testament to Maine shipbuilding skills and a challenge to the state that it move its maritime heritage even further ahead during better times after the Civil War.

While Portland flourished briefly as an invigorated seaport and rail depot and Bath as the center of by far the greatest state shipbuilding industry in the nation, Maine lumbering became centered at Bangor on the Penobscot. As early as 1833, the *Bangor Republican* was boasting that Maine furnished about three-fourths of all the white pine lumber exported from the United States and that the Penobscot River was in the middle of it. In 1836, the year after the great land boom during which the state land office sold 230,000 acres of public land at an average price of $1.45 an acre, there were more than 200 saws for boards alone in mills within a few miles of Bangor, mostly in Orono, "and a proportional number for laths, shingles and clapboards." On some days this enormous enterprise cut more than a million and a half board feet of lumber—a scale, one Massachusetts newspaper asserted, "which no one, who has never been 'down east,' can have an adequate conception of." [15] By 1842, the mills of Penobscot County were sawing over a hundred million board feet a year; the annual output reached its pre–Civil War peak in 1848, when the county produced 213,051,235 board feet of lumber, all of which was shipped through Bangor.

The land boom of 1835 ended almost as soon as it had begun, but the speculative fever remained. Land sales in northern and eastern Maine never again in that decade reached anything close to the level of the boom year, but the psychology of risk and expansive living gave to the raw city of Bangor a distinct aura of the West. The American frontier was pushing in two directions: Bangor, Maine, shared with Cincinnati, Ohio, and Independence, Missouri, the marks of newness, optimism, and recent growth. In 1846, the year the United States entered the war with Mexico that he opposed so bitterly, Henry David Thoreau made the first of three expeditions to Bangor and the Maine woods. "There stands the city of Bangor," he wrote, "fifty miles up the Penobscot, at the head of navigation for vessels of the larger class, the principal lumber depot on this continent, with a population of twelve thousand, like a star on the edge of the night, still hewing at the forest of which it is built, already overflowing with the luxuries and refinements of Europe, and sending its vessels to Spain, to England, and to the West Indies for its groceries—and yet only a few axe-men have gone 'up river,' into the howling wilderness which feeds it." [16]

By this time, the speculators on Maine lands were at it again, despite the presumed lessons of the Panic of 1837, of which land speculation in both Maine and the West had been the most conspicuous precursor. In 1849, public land sales in Maine actually surpassed those of 1835 in acreage, though not in dollars,

15. *Niles' Weekly Register* 50 (August 8, 1836): 378, quoting *Springfield Journal,* quoted in Wood, *Lumbering in Maine,* p. 36.

16. Henry David Thoreau, *The Maine Woods* (Boston, 1868), p. 83, quoted in Wood, *Lumbering in Maine,* p. 36.

and flourished spectacularly again in 1851 and 1852. Ironically, this is about the time the pine timber trade began to shift from the Penobscot to the new lumbering frontier in northern Wisconsin and Minnesota. And some Maine lumbermen began to go west, taking the logging techniques of the Maine woods to the virgin forests of the Great Lakes. Despite the shift, however, lumbering remained very much a part of Maine's economy, and remains so today. Bangor's good times stayed with her throughout the Civil War years and beyond. In 1866, 1868, 1871, and 1872, the amount of lumber surveyed at Bangor actually exceeded the 1848 total, but the emphasis shifted from pine to spruce, and eventually from boards to pulpwood.

Whatever one might say about continued prosperity, however, the "Bangor boom" really belongs to the frantically hustling thirties, forties, and early fifties. All Maine was looking ahead in those years, but in Bangor, the mood was especially intense and high-spirited. The streets were crowded with speculators, gamblers, sailors, builders, salesmen, opportunists, and adventurous men and women looking for each other. The waterfront was lined with grog shops, and they with seamen and, in the spring, loggers seeking the satiation of appetites built up during a winter in the woods and then climaxed by the dangerous drive down the Penobscot:

> When the Lumberman comes down,
> Ev'ry pocket bears a crown,
> And he wa-a-anders some pretty girl to find.
> If she's not too sly, with her dark and rolling eye,
> > The lumberman is pleased in his mind.
> > The lumberman is pleased in his mind.[17]

The humor of Bangor in these years was not the understated, comical, restrained wisdom of a Jack Downing, but the broad, exaggerated humor of the frontier. In 1835, the *Eastern Argus*

17. Fannie Hardy Eckstorm and Mary W. Smith, *Minstrelsy of Maine* (Boston and New York: Houghton Mifflin Co., 1927), pp. 96–97, quoted in David C. Smith, *A History of Lumbering in Maine, 1861–1960,* University of Maine Studies no. 93 (Orono, 1972), p. 67.

carried the amusing story of a sojourner in Bangor for whom it was hard to find a hotel room in the crowded city, so he paid seventy-five cents for room to lean against a sign post. In five years, the story had grown to the point that the tenant of the sign post was selling his leaning space for five dollars a crack. Or take this whopper from the *Newburyport Herald:* "It is rumored that one evening last week, two paupers escaped from the Bangor almshouse, and though they were caught early the next morning, yet in the meantime, before they were secured, they had made $1,800 each, by speculating in timber lands." [18]

It was this Bangor that the Maine novelist Ben Ames Williams described a hundred years later in informed historical fiction:

> June came booming up the river, and life in Bangor was on the flood. Every packet brought a new flood of speculators and potential citizens. . . . Hundreds of houses and store buildings and new wharves were everywhere under way. The streets had been churned to a quagmire as the frost went out of the ground, and there had been no time nor inclination to scrape and level them. . . . The mud turned to dust and back to mud again with every rain, and the heavy teams hauling lumber and rock and brick for construction work churned holes which there was never time to fill. Footpaths by the roadside were the only sidewalks, and in the busy streets these disappeared so that pedestrians picked their way along in front of the stores, forever dodging teams or carriages, crossing where they could.
>
> And everywhere, at street corners, in the taverns, wherever two men met, the trading went on and paper passed from hand to hand. There was a current of excitement in the air so intense that most men were infected; and the fever in their blood burned so hot that they might stay all night at the Coffee House or at one of the other taverns or at John Bright's news room, in endless talks of what had been and what might be. [19]

18. *Niles' Weekly Register* 48 (June 27, 1835): 291, quoting *Newburyport Herald,* quoted in Wood, *Lumbering in Maine,* p. 79.

19. Ben Ames Williams, *The Strange Woman* (Cambridge, Mass.: Houghton Mifflin Co., 1943), pp. 221–222.

Shipbuilders, railroad promoters, lumbermen, and land speculators: In the giddy decades between statehood and the Civil War, all talked of what might be. On nearly every side, it seemed that the future belonged very much to the new State of Maine.

7

General Dow, Antislavery,
and the Holy Ghost

N the thirties, forties, and fifties, the raw wood bustle of Bangor gave that booming Penobscot town the look and feel of quick money. It also gave it something of a reputation for sin. The town had lumbermen, seamen, gamblers, drinking places, and whores. Frontier towns in boom days, West or East, have rarely been known for restraint.

But there were those in Maine who had the feeling that hard drinking and loose living were far too distinctive a mark, not just of Bangor, but of the whole state. Neal Dow, who felt that way more than anyone, gave some examples in the fascinating if somewhat pompous life of himself that he wrote at the end of a long career of reform. He wrote of a village grog shop and country store in Kennebec County in the 1840s, attracting "a poor set of fellows, half laborers and two-thirds loafers," who "hung around the village, whetting their appetite for rum with crackers and codfish, their chief articles of diet." He quoted the report of a country doctor of the same era that in Fryeburg, "There are now in this village twenty widows whose husbands were killed by drink." And he remarked on an investigating committee's finding in 1840 that Portland held "five hundred common drunkards in a population of about twelve thousand.'' [1]

Nobody can accuse Neal Dow of inaction when he saw what needed to be done. Almost single-handedly, this strong-minded, Quaker-born crusader led the fight for temperance until on May 30, 1851, when he was mayor of Portland, the state legislature passed the bill he had written banishing booze from the State of Maine. By 1855, twelve other states and one territory had followed with prohibition statutes modeled after Neal Dow's famous ''Maine Law.''

Here was a man with his own image of Maine. It was an image born in a Quaker boyhood, nurtured by the reform enthusiasm abroad in American life in the tumultuous twenties and thirties, and confirmed by his own vision, exaggerated though it may have been, of the Maine he saw around him during the exciting days when most eyes were fixed on economic growth. Neal Dow and John Poor were looking at the same places, and even at the same men—and were aware of the same forces at work in society and of similar possibilities. For Poor, the resulting vision was promise. For Dow, it was danger.

And it was not just an image of sin and dissipation. Neal Dow had a theory, too—a theory about Maine's past and future. One might call it the alcoholic interpretation of history.

In the beginning, wrote Dow, Maine had been ''rich in material resources, as yet all undeveloped and mostly undiscovered.'' Forests, rivers, bays, and fish combined to create vast potential wealth for any who would settle and work diligently to exploit them. It was a good start and the settlers came, but Maine suffered badly during the wars with the Indians and during the two wars with Britain. In the War of 1812, in fact, ''It has been claimed that, in proportion to her population, the district furnished more soldiers to that war than did any state.'' If that claim is true, then ''Maine had a larger proportion of men without families than any other portion of the Union.'' Not only had the War of 1812 disrupted commerce and

1. Neal Dow, *The Reminiscences of Neal Dow* (Portland, Me.: Evening Express Publishing Co., 1898), pp. 175–176.

interrupted normal work and family life, "but so large a proportion of the male population was for longer or shorter periods in
camp, that habits contracted there came subsequently to exert a
marked influence upon the entire community." That was the
nub of the matter. Habits contracted in camp, reinforced by the
trade by which Maine had tried to emerge from the disaster of
the embargo and the war: the classic pattern of New England fish
and lumber for West Indian rum.[2]

Intemperance and its evil consequences ran highest in the
three decades after statehood, according to Dow's exhaustive
analysis. And those drunken decades, he believed, took an enormous toll. The state was poorer then than any other in the
Union. The cause was obvious. Combining his own researches
and observations with the recollections of others, Dow came up
with a picture of a countryside filled with neglected farms and
dilapidated buildings, and of seaside towns filled on Saturday
nights with drunken, fighting shipyard workers and visiting
farmers from the nearby countryside.

"At the time of the admission of Maine to the Union and for
thirty years thereafter," Dow concluded, "her people probably
consumed more intoxicating liquor in proportion to their
numbers than the people of any other state."[3] Logging and
fishing, Maine's two leading industries, kept men away from
the "restraining, conserving and elevating influences" of home
life and exposed them to temptation. Liquor was a normal part
of the lumberman's and fisherman's daily rations because it was
thought to be "a panacea for all complaints, a protection in all
forms of exposure, a relief for fatigue and pain" and the other
discomforts of hard work and extreme temperatures. "The excitement of drink took the place of the comforts of life," and
"excess naturally followed." During the off-seasons back in
towns and villages, the loggers and fishermen kept on drinking,
"and the 'stay-at-homes' vied in dissipation with the men who
had returned from work in the woods or on the sea. The boys
imitated their elders, until indulgence in drink almost every-

2. Dow, *Reminiscences*, pp. 152–155.
3. Dow, *Reminiscences*, p. 167.

where was the rule. These habits spread easily because there was no opposing public opinion." [4]

In view of the great reformer's acute analysis of the causes of drunkenness, which seems to have included a reasonably humane and sympathetic understanding of the dangers and hardships faced by much of the state's work force, the modern reader is perhaps taken aback by the strident moralism that marks much of Dow's writing and action. It is not, however, that he was unaware of root causes, nor that he could not perhaps have thought of more fundamental reforms. But to his stern and searching eyes, the one link in the chain of dissipation and poverty that the law could easily strike was the rum bottle. Moreover, there was simply no doubt in his mind that "the liquor-traffic . . . was a chief contributing cause of the poor condition of the state at the lowest point of its material prosperity." [5] If this was not yet a moral issue, very well then, it must become a moral issue—for by a logic that has not necessarily stood the test of time, immorality was believed to precede illegality. And so Neal Dow devoted his considerable strengths to bringing moderate drinkers and occasional rowdies under the same public scrutiny and censure that had been reserved up to then for confirmed drunkards. The law, he thought, would then follow. Boosted along by important alliances, shrewd politics, and temperance tracts, it did.

Temperance agitation in Maine had begun before Dow reached adulthood, concentrated largely in a few of the churches and led principally by clergymen. By 1837, when Dow was thirty-three, the Maine Temperance Union had bolted from its more moderate parent group, the Maine Temperance Society, on a platform of total abstinence. At its first meeting the new union voted to discuss the possibility of petitioning the legislature for a prohibition law. The next year, the Whigs snapped a long string of Democratic election victories in a state that had been traditionally Democratic ever since the break from Massachusetts in 1820, putting Edward Kent, a bone-dry confidant

4. Dow, *Reminiscences*, p. 169.
5. Dow, *Reminiscences*, p. 180.

of Neal Dow's, into the governor's chair. Dow, active in the Temperance Union and a member of the governor's staff, now began to lead the long fight for prohibition.

He went about his task like an evangelist; indeed, for him this was a religious as well as a social cause. His memoirs bristle with words like "revival," "reformation," "conversion," and "convert." Concentrating first on his home city of Portland, he held great public meetings in which he got hundreds to "sign the pledge" of lifelong personal abstinence. But "moral suasion," as it was called, was only the first step. What to Dow and a growing body of followers was a moral principle must now, for the public good, be embodied into law. His first personal triumph came in 1842, when he got enough signatures on a petition to persuade the city's sympathetic aldermen to withhold all liquor licenses that year. When the former licensees continued to sell their wares anyway, Dow and his followers engineered a public referendum, in which the vote was 943 to 498 for cracking down on illegal sales.

Having won an impressive victory on the local level, Dow now set his sights with new zeal on the state. This larger crusade came to a climax in 1846, when Dow and another representative of the Temperance Union presented to a legislative hearing a fifty-nine-foot petition for prohibition bearing 3,800 signatures. That was the year the legislature overwhelmingly adopted the first prohibition law—the first, Dow exulted, ever passed by "a civilized and Christian state." [6] The "Act to Restrict the Sale of Intoxicating Drinks" outlawed the sale of liquor except for medicinal and "mechanical" purposes. Dow was ecstatic, but soon found that it was rather a poor law. Big loopholes and tiny teeth, even with subsequent attempts to fill gaps here and there with supplementary laws, rendered the 1846 law ineffective. Dow became mayor of Portland in early 1851, and was itching to enforce the law against liquor. To do it effec-

6. John Marsh, *The Napoleon of Temperance: Sketches on the Life and Character of Neal Dow* (New York: American Temperance Union, 1852), p. 7, quoted by Charles A. Jellison in *Fessenden of Maine: Civil War Senator* (Syracuse, N.Y.: Syracuse University Press, 1962), p. 54.

tively, he needed a better law. The "Maine Law" of 1851, supported by hundreds of petitions, was his own creation. With literature, petitions, conferences with the president of the senate and speaker of the house, who then packed the committees in Dow's favor, and intensive lobbying, Dow went to work in behalf of his "Act for the Suppression of Drinking Houses and Tippling Shops." Dow himself took the signed bill from the house to the senate and from the senate to Gov. John Hubbard. Hubbard was a Democrat, and some of the legislative leaders of his own party worked hard on him to veto it. But Hubbard, who had never been active either in the temperance movement or in the affairs of the party, earned Dow's gratitude and lasting respect by signing the bill on June 2. The act contained elaborate provisions for enforcement and specified stiff penalties. Dow's dream was the law of the state, and his image of Maine would now improve immensely.

Neal Dow's vision of degradation and poverty, and his twin prescriptions of evangelical temperance and legal prohibition, remain the most conspicuous and only really indigenous way in which the new state participated in the outburst of reform enthusiasm that flourished throughout the North during the three decades before the Civil War. But it was far from the only way. These years were precisely the ones during which Maine was finding her identity, searching her future, and bewailing her sins. Her very birth had been bound up with the festering controversy over extending slavery, and the character of her infancy was shaped almost as much by a pervasive climate of moral and social reform as by optimistic visions of future prosperity. In fact, Neal Dow's Franklinesque assertion of the relationship between drunkenness and poverty (and temperance and prosperity) is the best illustration that these two dominant attitudes during Maine's formative period as a state were far from incompatible. It may be that by some perverse social psychology that intertwined guilt over the Missouri Compromise with self-righteousness, Mainers subconsciously felt that of the two very conspicuous new states in the Union (there was not another after Missouri until 1836), theirs as the "free" and therefore progressive half of the pair had a special duty to lead national opinion

by example. Was this not, in fact, the message implicit in
Dirigo ("I lead"), the state motto adopted by the first legislature? [7]

The abolition movement came to Maine, where there had
been no slaves (and almost no free blacks) at least since the
Massachusetts Constitution of 1780, almost at the moment of
statehood. The Missouri Compromise had involved primarily
the issue of permitting the spread of slavery and the concern
over a sectional balance in the Senate. These debates led immediately to a fight over slavery itself. The first antislavery sermon
in Maine to receive a wide hearing was probably the one given
by Asa Cummings at Bowdoin in April 1820, less than a month
after the admission of the new state. The antislavery sentiments
of this young Bowdoin tutor, though moderate by the standards
of the next decade, were vigorously expressed and apparently
appealed to the students, at whose request the sermon was
printed. The Reverend Mr. Cummings, however, was a gradua-
list and a colonizationist; he believed, that is, that a free inter-
racial society was not possible and that the right approach to
ending slavery was to provide a means by which freedmen
could be relocated in Africa. He later became editor of the
Christian Mirror, a Portland Congregational weekly that served
as the Maine voice of the American Colonization Society, the
principal sponsor of that approach. But colonization obviously
would take time, and neither that nor the emancipation of future
colonists could be done all at once. Therefore, to a more militant corps of abolitionists that arose in the 1830s, colonization
and gradualism meant a compromise with evil—aimed, in fact,

7. Actually, the legislative committee that reported the proposed device for the seal
and arms of the new state claimed that the North Star in the crest was intended to repre-
sent the state, which in turn was to "be considered the citizen's guide, and the object to
which the patriot's best exertions should be directed." Hence the motto *"Dirigo,"*
meaning "I guide," or "I direct." When out-of-state criticism suggested that the motto
was pretentious, the *Eastern Argus* pointed out the committee's report, observing that
the state claimed to lead only her own citizens, not the other states. Few readers of the
motto, in Maine or out, then or since, have really believed that. See, e.g., Louis Clinton
Hatch, *Maine: A History* (1919; reprint ed., Somersworth, N.H.: New Hampshire Publishing Co., 1974), pp. 171–172.

not so much at ridding the country of slaves as at ridding it of free Negroes. The sin of slavery, they held, must be abolished at once; the American Colonization Society stood in the way of this aim.

The apostle of immediate abolition who came to Maine to do battle with the *Christian Mirror* and the gradualists was none other than William Lloyd Garrison himself, militant editor of the *Liberator* and the fiercest abolitionist of them all. Garrison toured Maine in the autumn of 1832, making converts and allies in Portland, Hallowell, Bangor, Waterville College (later Colby), and finally Augusta, where the tour climaxed dramatically with a face-to-face confrontation with the Reverend Cyril Pearl, an agent of the Colonization Society who had come to Maine specifically to fight the influence of Garrison. The students at Waterville, where Garrison was entertained by Pres. Jeremiah Chapin, formed an antislavery society in July 1833, about the same time that the debate between Maine Garrisonians and the advocates of colonization reached a heated climax and a turning point. From then on, Maine leaned toward militant abolitionism, led principally by Gen. Samuel Fessenden of Portland, a close friend of Garrison and a vice-president of the American Antislavery Society. The state movement was institutionalized first in a string of local antislavery societies and finally in the Maine Antislavery Society, founded at Augusta in October 1834. Reflecting both the religious and moral basis of abolitionist agitation in the 1830s and the uncompromising position of the Garrisonian wing of the movement, the Maine society's constitution declared:

> The fundamental principles of this society are that slave-holding is a heinous sin against God, and therefore that immediate emancipation without the condition of expatriation is the duty of the master and the right of the slave.[8]

The shift from "moral suasion" to political action on the slavery issue came with the founding in 1841 of the Maine Liberty party. Like most single-issue parties in American politics,

8. Quoted by Edward O. Schriver in *Go Free: The Antislavery Impulse in Maine, 1833–1855*, University of Maine Studies no. 91 (Orono, 1970), p. 10.

this one had little success—none at all in electing its candidates to office. In the hectic political year of 1848, therefore, the leaders of the Liberty party threw in their lot with the Free-Soilers. In this way, because of the new party's strong appeal to all of the reform-minded in Maine, the abolitionists were brought into firm political alliance with the temperance men.

Not that the connection was an unnatural one. Neal Dow, though obsessed by the fight against booze to the extent that other concerns were subordinate, nevertheless pronounced himself "earnestly antislavery in my convictions, and irrevocably opposed to the extension of the peculiar institution." [9] Other temperance men less single-minded than Dow gravitated naturally to the great national reform movement of the day without compromising their views on alcohol, and in Maine, at least, an antislavery man was likely also to sympathize with the temperance movement—if he were not right in the middle of it.

But that is how the reform impulse was everywhere. Inspired by evangelical religion, a vision of the future greatness of America, oriental philosophy, economic vibrancy, the grim and growing sectional divisions, and probably a few other things that historians have yet to put their fingers on, the American people went wild with causes and enthusiasms. And the causes and movements overlapped and intertwined. Besides abolition, the central cause with which all reformers sympathized, there were women's rights, school reform, prison reform, a peace movement, utopian communities ranging from the celibate Shakers to the promiscuous sharers in "complex marriage" at John Humphrey Noyes's Oneida Community in New York State, opponents of white bread, spiritualists and phrenologists who got messages from angels or solemnly examined the bumps on one another's heads, thumping evangelists like Charles Grandison Finney, and a variety of new religious sects from Joseph Smith's Mormons to the followers of William Miller, who on October 22, 1843, having sold all their worldly goods, stood in white robes waiting in vain for the Second Coming.

A native of Hamden, Maine, Dorothea Dix, waged a success-

9. Dow, *Reminiscences*, p. 502.

ful one-woman campaign for hospitals for the insane in Massachusetts; the idea soon spread to several other states and to Canada and Europe. From his farm in Minot, Maine, William Ladd publicized his plan for an international government and founded and presided over the American Peace Society. On November 7, 1837, a thirty-five-year-old Waterville College graduate who had grown up in the Unitarian parsonage in Albion, Maine, was shot by a mob in Alton, Illinois. Elijah Parish Lovejoy, editor of the *Alton Observer*, died as he stood by his printing press for offending the mob by repeatedly opposing slavery and calling for more law and order in Illinois and Missouri.

In Maine itself, anti-Masonry rode high in the 1830s. In the fifties, Roman Catholics and "foreigners" were a more popular target. The Know-Nothings (most of whom supported both abolition and prohibition) burned a Catholic church in Bath and tarred and feathered an Ellsworth priest who had dared protest the school committee's requirement that the children of his French parishioners read the Protestant version of the Bible in school.

And on a Sunday morning in February 1851, frail Harriet Beecher Stowe, five months short of her fortieth birthday, attended a Communion service at the First Parish Church of Brunswick and had a vision. The conversation of the nation had been full of the Compromise of 1850, and New England was accusing Daniel Webster of betrayal for agreeing to a stronger Fugitive Slave law. In New York City, the capture of Henry Long and his return to his southern claimants by a federal judge had raised the hackles of handsome young Henry Ward Beecher, Harriet's marvelously successful younger brother, who for some time now had been using his pulpit at the Plymouth Congregational Church in Brooklyn as an abolitionist platform. Early in January 1851, Henry had visited his sister in Brunswick during a lecture trip to Boston, and the two had sat up all night talking about slavery and the Fugitive Slave Law and their plans to fight both. Harriet had lived close to slavery during her eighteen years in Cincinnati, a bustling Ohio River port near the South where slavetraders gathered and the newspapers carried advertisements for runaways from Kentucky plantations. There her father, the famous Lyman Beecher from Connecticut, and the man she married, Calvin Stowe, had served as two-thirds of the faculty at Lane Theological Seminary. She had also recently met in Boston a kindly and forgiving black minister who years before had been crippled for life in a brutal beating by a master.

Now as Harriet contemplated the mysteries of Christ's suffering and sacrifice during that Brunswick Communion service, she saw "almost as a tangible vision" an old black slave being flogged to death by two younger slaves while a cruel white master looked on. In the same scene, the dying slave, his body bathed in blood, prayed forgiveness for his oppressors. Here were born Uncle Tom, and Quimbo and Sambo, and Simon Legree, the wicked Yankee slaveholder. Home Harriet went to the marvelous white house overlooking Federal and Maine streets on the edge of the Bowdoin campus to write the climactic scene of what would become *Uncle Tom's Cabin,* just as she had seen it in church:

> Legree drew in a long breath; and, suppressing his rage, took Tom by the arm, and, approaching his face almost to his, said in a terrible voice, "Hark 'e Tom! . . . *I'll conquer ye or kill ye!*—one or t'other. I'll count every drop of blood there is in you, and take 'em, one by one, till ye give up!"
>
> Tom looked up to his master, "Mas'r, if you was sick, or in trouble, or dying, and I could save ye, I'd *give* ye my heart's blood; and, if taking every drop of blood in this poor old body would save your precious soul, I'd give 'em freely, as the Lord gave his for me. Oh, Mas'r! don't bring this great sin on your soul! . . . my troubles 'll be over soon; but, if ye don't repent, yours won't *never* end!"

Legree, of course, goes ahead with the flogging, enlisting Quimbo and Sambo to do the dreadful deed:

> "He's most gone, Mas'r," said Sambo, touched, in spite of himself, by the patience of his victim.
>
> "Pay away, till he gives up! Give it to him!—give it to him!" shouted Legree. . . .
>
> Tom opened his eyes, and looked upon his master. "Ye poor

miserable crittur!'' he said, ''there an't no more ye can do! I
forgive ye, with all my soul!'' and he fainted entirely away.[10]

Tom soon dies, but not before forgiving Quimbo and Sambo
and after some hasty religious instruction, converting them both
to Christianity.

Calvin Stowe, detained in Cincinnati while his wife set up
housekeeping in Brunswick, joined her a month later to take up
a new Bowdoin professorship. He read the scene in tears, and
urged his wife to ''make up a story with this for the climax. The
Lord intends it so.'' [11]

On June 5, 1851, *Uncle Tom's Cabin, or Life Among the
Lowly* began its serialized run in the *National Era,* a Washington antislavery weekly that had already published some of Mrs.
Stowe's pieces. It was an immediate sensation. The first edition
in book form came out on March 20, 1852; in a year, it sold
305,000 copies in the United States alone and about two and a
half million in several languages around the world. Mrs. Stowe
of Brunswick had become a world figure, and *Uncle Tom's
Cabin,* along with *Dred: A Tale of The great Dismal Swamp,*
which she wrote in 1856, probably did more for the struggle
against slavery than all the antislavery societies combined. Indeed, a very great man attributed even greater influence to her
than that. In November 1862, soon after the Battle of Antietam
(in which four Maine regiments had fought) and the preliminary
Emancipation Proclamation, Mrs. Stowe visited Washington.
''So this,'' Abraham Lincoln remarked when she called at the
White House, ''is the little lady who made this big war.'' [12]

The exclusive role of Mrs. Stowe's book in bringing on the
Civil War may well be doubted, even though the observation is
reported to have come from Honest Abe himself. But this Maine
author certainly contributed more than her share to the rising in-

10. Harriet Beecher Stowe, *Uncle Tom's Cabin* (Boston, n.d., Riverside Library
ed.), pp. 461–462.

11. Forrest Wilson, *Crusader in Crinoline: The Life of Harriet Beecher Stowe* (Philadelphia: J. B. Lippincott Co., 1941), p. 257.

12. Wilson, *Crusader in Crinoline,* p. 484.

tersectional tensions of the fifties. So did the state's most prominent politicians.

With the virtual collapse of the Whig party in the forties and the end with the Compromise of 1850 of the immediate cause that had given birth to the Free-Soil party, most of the reformist elements in Maine and elsewhere were attracted into combination with many of the former Whigs and certain sectional and business interests in the new Republican party. The Maine Republicans, drawing support from antislavery Democrats as well as from Whigs, Free-Soilers, and Know-Nothings, organized themselves in 1854, only a month after the formation of the national party. Campaigning on a strong antislavery platform and in defense of the existing prohibition law, they captured the governor's chair the very first time out. They lost it to the Democrats in the next election, but by the crucial presidential election year of 1860, the party not only was dominating Maine politics but also contained some of the biggest political names in the history of the state before or since. There was Gov. Anson P. Morrill, the first Republican governor, now back in office again for the past several terms. There was Sen. William Pitt Fessenden, elected as a Whig in 1854 by a coalition of antislavery and temperance men in the Democrat-controlled Maine legislature, an early convert to the Republican party during his first term in the Senate. There was Senator Hannibal Hamlin, a former Democrat converted to Republicanism because of his antislavery sympathies, who served briefly as governor in 1856 before resigning to accept appointment to the Senate. And there was James G. Blaine, editor of the influential *Kennebec Journal* of Augusta and a founder of the Maine Republican party. At this point, Blaine, future Speaker of the House, secretary of state, and presidential candidate, had hardly begun his long and stormy political career.

In 1860, both Fessenden and Hamlin were being mentioned for the Republican presidential nomination. Fessenden steadfastly refused to allow his name to be brought up at the Chicago convention. Hamlin and Blaine were early and strong supporters of Lincoln; Morrill, who went to the convention with Blaine, became a Lincoln partisan after he got there. The convention nominated Lincoln and Hamlin of Maine as his running mate. The election of Lincoln and Hamlin that fall in an election that followed regional lines set in motion the machinery of Southern secession. The political giants of Maine shared an eerie complicity in this grim chain of events.

Once war came, the communities of Maine responded at least as enthusiastically as any other part of the North in providing companies and regiments of soldiers. For this state as for several others in the North, the Civil War was a crusade—even though it was not until 1863 that it officially became a struggle against slavery. In all, something like 67,000 Maine men served in the thirty-five Maine regiments, special units, or Navy and Marine Corps during the four years of war. Almost 9,000 of them died, and another 11,000 were disabled by wounds or sickness. Maine contributed ten infantry regiments, a cavalry regiment, three artillery batteries and a company of sharpshooters to the 93,000-man Federal force under Gen. George Gordon Meade that turned back Robert E. Lee at Gettysburg, by that feat spelling the doom of the Confederacy.

Maine's highest ranking military leaders of the Civil War leaned heavily toward educators and reformers. Col. Joshua L. Chamberlain of Brewer, a former language professor at Bowdoin, commanded the Twentieth Maine Infantry, which held the line at Little Round Top on the second day of Gettysburg. Later, as a major general, he was named by Ulysses S. Grant to command the contingent of Union troops that accepted the surrender of the Confederate army. After the war, he served four times as governor of Maine, and then became president of Bowdoin. Late in life, both he and Brig. Gen. Oliver Curtis Howard of Leeds, a Bowdoin man and West Pointer who commanded the entire right wing of Sherman's march through Georgia, were voted the Medal of Honor. Howard went on to head the Freedmen's Bureau during Reconstruction, to found Howard University and serve as its first president, to serve as superintendent of West Point, and to found Lincoln Memorial University in Tennessee. Chamberlain's predecessor as commander of the Twentieth Maine, Col. Adelbert Ames of Rockland, later a major general, served as Reconstruction governor of Mississippi. Neal

Dow, the temperance crusader, was commissioned to raise the
Thirteenth Maine Infantry Regiment. He accepted the job on
condition that he be allowed to appoint his own officers, based
on good character and abstemious habits. Reluctant mothers of
military-age boys were content in some cases to let their sons
enlist after all, as long as it could be in Neal Dow's "Prohibition Regiment." It was an encampment of the Thirteenth from
which a rum peddler was driven at bayonet point. There, too,
according to Dow's own account, "Every evening at dress
parade, so long as I remained with the regiment, there were
religious exercises, singing and prayers before the parade was
dismissed. . . . I was anxious to show, and did so to my satisfaction, that brutality, coarseness, drunkenness, profanity and
other vices common in camp life were not necessary to make
good soldiers." [13] The Thirteenth served to good effect in the
western theater. Dow was promoted to brigadier general and
commanded a brigade in several battles until he was wounded
and captured in 1863. After eight months in a Confederate
prison, he was exchanged for a Southern general. He returned to
Maine a military hero, to fight the temperance war once again.

The crusade against slavery was certainly the dominant mood
in Maine at the outbreak of the war, but there were those who
dissented. Abolition sentiment had never been unanimous, and
now that the break was at hand, it was especially painful for
those whose living came from shipbuilding or from transatlantic
trade. Ever since 1820, the business of shipping cotton from the
Gulf Coast to England had been a staple of Maine commerce,
and had been a chief stimulus to Maine shipbuilding. Maine
shipping agents had taken up residence in New Orleans; some
southern merchants had bought shares in Maine-built ships and
hired Maine skippers. In a few instances, intersectional business
connections had resulted in intersectional marriages. For the
merchants, builders, and families involved in such connections,
the question of abolition had always been at best ambiguous.
For them, war was a disaster. This turned out to be even more
the case—though loyalty to cause and to section was made that

13. Dow, *Reminiscences,* p. 667.

much easier—when a handful of highly successful Confederate commerce raiders began to capture and burn Yankee shipping. The *Alabama* captured 386 vessels, including eleven from Maine, before the U.S.S. *Kearsarge,* built at the Portsmouth Navy Yard in Kittery, sunk her off Cherbourg, France, on June 12, 1864. The *Tallahassee,* another Confederate cruiser, captured seventeen Maine vessels alone. Four other cruisers took eleven Maine ships among them—one, the Bangor bark *Delphine,* in the middle of the Indian Ocean! Confederate Navy Lt. Charles W. Read, shifting his twenty-man crew from captured ship to captured ship as he worked his way north in the spring of 1863, ended up in Portland Harbor, where he blew up the Federal revenue cutter *Caleb Cushing* before a makeshift naval force organized by the mayor finally took him into custody.

All in all, the war cost Maine dearly—in 9,000 lives, in $18 million appropriated to raise and support troops, and in the near ruin of the state's ocean commerce. For reformers and politicians, however, this was the culmination of the great reform impulse of which Neal Dow's crusade against liquor was the special Maine manifestation. For them, crusaders that they were, the defeat of the South was worth the cost. Was it worth it to those who suffered most personally—the bereaved, the maimed, those in split families? It is too late to ask them.

The intensity of reforming zeal in the antebellum years, and the sense of sin that informed it, found a special hospitality and a special nourishment in the religious atmosphere of the state. Entirely secular in origin, the settlements of Maine had provided a place of early refuge for sectaries who failed to find a hospitable home in Massachusetts. Almost always, these people favored the subjective, the mystical, and the unstructured varieties of religious expression. Antinomians, Quakers, and Baptists all found their way to Maine in the seventeenth century. Then in the era of Cotton Mather came the Puritanization of Maine, only partly successful. During the Great Awakening, a few decades after that, it was the "New Light" side of the controversy that carried the day in most of the seacoast towns. And when new churches were set up in the countryside between the Great Awakening and the American Revolution, they tended to follow the evangelical emphases of the revival, resulting in a swarm of Baptist churches and radical, anti-Calvinist Congregational churches that easily slipped over into Universalism after the Revolution. At the same time, the anti-Calvinist rebellion promoted the rise of the Free Will Baptists, who in the nineteenth century became vehemently active in the antislavery movement and founded Bates College and Maine Central Institute. In the 1790s, Methodism came to Maine, and this anti-Calvinist and enthusiastic sect soon rivaled the Baptists for the affections of the plain and humble Mainers of the countryside, where neither the dignified Massachusetts-style Congregationalism of the seaboard nor its sophisticated offshoot Unitarianism had much appeal.

So by about the time of statehood, the majority of Maine believers—which does not count a great many people who never bothered much with religion at all—tended to be either rough-and-ready evangelicals like the Methodists and Baptists (most of whom were also Democrats) or introspective souls like the Quakers who pondered the Inner Light while doing good and spawning the next generation's reformers. Maine Congregationalism, like that in Massachusetts, tended to be allied with Federalism and the political and social status quo. But even that did not last long. Swept up in the reform movement and obeying the logic of their own liberalized Calvinist theology, Maine Congregationalists zealously set about doing good by trying to rid the world of slaves and alcohol, meanwhile inventing the conference system of co-operative church government, which was soon adopted by Congregationalists throughout the nation, and establishing an itinerant ministry to the back parts through the Maine Missionary Society. As early as 1814, they had founded Bangor Theological Seminary, right in the future city of sin.

The enthusiastic and introspective qualities that came to dominate much of Maine religious life found peculiar expression in an especially fascinating sect that was not confined to Maine, but which nevertheless occupies too conspicuous a place on the Maine landscape to ignore. The sect's official name is The

United Society of Believers in Christ's Second Coming; its popular name, the Shakers. "Mother" Ann Lee of Manchester, England, bouncing back from a bad marriage, proclaimed a bisex-
ual god, of which she embodied the "female principle." Thus
taking charge of a Quaker splinter group that had already begun
taking shape, this illiterate, mystical, frustrated woman outlawed sexual intercourse among her followers and led a group to
America in 1774. She set up Shaker communes at Watervliet
and then New Lebanon, New York; for the next fifty years,
offshoots spread out over the American countryside from Maine
to Indiana. By 1843, the sect's membership had reached 6,000.
After New Lebanon, Maine had one of the earliest Shaker communities, the one that as of 1977 still carries on with a few celibate brothers and sisters who make and sell things to 10,000
tourists each summer at Sabbathday Lake. There were two other
communities in the state, one at Gorham, which soon merged
with the Sabbathday Lake community, and one at Alfred, which
lasted from 1793 to 1931.

Life in a Maine Shaker community, apart from the world at
large though it was, was not at all ethereal except during those
ecstatic moments when the community cultivated transcendence. Delmar Wilson joined the Sabbathday Lake community
in 1882 at age eight. When he died in 1961, he left a diary. The
record of his teen-age years includes occasional references to
"good meetings," but the day-to-day life he described in 1887,
when he was thirteen, was at least as much Maine as Shaker. In
school, he was obliged to write a composition entitled "Why
not keep your mouth shut," but the next day, a Saturday, "us
boys was down to the barn and we put up a swing and had some
fun." He seems to have been the village specialist in trying to
"learn a calf to drink." He planted "limer beans," "lugged
sixty quarts of water" to the barn-bound cows one wintry day,
and was once kept from Sunday night meeting by a wandering
and apparently incomplete cow named Three-Tits.[14]

14. "The Diary of a Maine Shaker Boy: Delmar Wilson—1887," ed. Theodore E.
Johnson, *The Shaker Quarterly* 8 (Spring 1968): 3–22.

The ceremonial heart of the Shaker communal life, however, was something else again. One observer described the climax of a service in the Alfred community in 1903 as follows:

> In chorus the brothers began a hymn and led a circling march in column, two abreast, the sisters following in sections, three abreast. In the march was a waving movement of the hands by drawing them inward and occasionally all clapped hands in perfect concert, repeating in resounding rounds. As they marched and countermarched the worshippers frequently changed positions. . . . Leading singers stood in the center and the others encircled them twice in marching. Eventually the major body formed in single file and made four circles, symbolical of the four great dispensations expounded by Shakerism. In conclusion the audience stood silent and then quietly left the church, men and women making their exit by designated doors.[15]

Throughout most of its history, therefore, Maine has furnished a setting for the kind of folk who like to set themselves apart from the world for ecstatic communion with higher realms. Perhaps there is something about the stark landscapes of Maine that is especially conducive to experiences like that described by Rufus Jones, the famous Quaker mystic of South China, Maine, in which "the walls between the visible and the invisible grow thin."[16] Whatever the explanation, Maine not only played host to visiting cults and dreamers, but furnished several homegrown varieties as well. Rufus Jones, who died in 1948 full of years and the world's respect, was one of them. Another was Frank W. Sandford, a native of Bowdoinham, a graduate of Bates, a college and professional baseball catcher, and a Free Will Baptist preacher who quit the regular Baptist ministry in 1893 to become a free-lance evangelist and founder of the World's Evangelization Crusade on Apostolic Principles, later known as "The Holy Ghost and Us Society." Sandford, like the Mormons' Joseph Smith, had visions. In one, he was

15. *Lewiston Journal,* quoted by Edward F. Dow in *A Portrait of the Millennial Church of Shakers,* University of Maine Studies no. 19 (Orono, 1931), p. 16.

16. Gloria Hutchinson, "Rufus M. Jones—Maine Quaker Mystic," *Down East* 22 (June 1976): 58.

instructed to build a temple for his followers. So in 1896, on a hill in Durham, Maine, Sandford and his converts broke ground for the remarkable community of Shiloh. The four-story, white building in gold trim and with a gilt-domed, five-story tower called the "Eye of the Needle," was dedicated on the Fourth of July, 1897. During the next eight years, residential and classroom buildings, a children's home, and a hospital were added to this spiritual commune, upon entry to which each convert gave up all possessions and followed a life of strict personal discipline—while Sandford, calling himself "Elijah," owned more than seventy horses and rode in a white chariot, which he replaced after a time with a purple Cadillac. In 1910, Sandford sailed from South Freeport as commodore of a two-ship expedition bound on a crusade for world evangelization. He tried his luck on the coast of Africa, but when the tribesmen only laughed at him, he burned one of his ships, the *Kingdom,* as a sacrificial offering for the salvation of Africa. All sixty-six crew members and fellow evangelists then crowded aboard the *Coronet,* the remaining ship, for a half-starved odyssey about the Atlantic that touched both Haiti and Greenland and finally ended in Portland Harbor. Eight members of the expedition had died from various causes, for which Sandford was convicted in a federal court of manslaughter. He served part of a ten-year term in Atlanta Federal Penitentiary while the movement declined. After his release in 1918, he returned to a much quieter Shiloh, which began—and continues—to erect barriers of secrecy against the curious. He died in Florida in 1948. His followers insist that the reason nobody can find his grave is that he ascended into heaven as any proper Elijah ought to do.

It could, one supposes, be the Maine air. It has, after all, been accused of almost as many things as it has been praised for, and has even been canned and sold in gift shops. It certainly nourished Edwin Arlington Robinson, an exceptionally gifted Maine mystic of the same generation as Sanford's. Robinson was born to the general storekeeper of Head Tide and his wife on December 22, 1869. He didn't trust knowledge like Sandford's, the kind that knew all about the Holy Ghost and built gilt-domed towers. He cared even less about the kind that tells us all we need to know of nature and the world. His central poem, *The Man Against the Sky* (1916) really says at the end that such knowledge is hollow:

> If after all that we have lived and thought,
> All comes to Nought,—
> If there be nothing after Now,
> And we be nothing anyhow,
> And we know that,—why live?
> 'Twere sure but weaklings' vain distress
> To suffer dungeons where so many doors
> Will open on the cold eternal shores
> That look sheer down
> To the dark tideless floods of Nothingness
> Where all who know may drown.

And yet Maine's greatest poet thought there might be a better answer to the puzzle of existence than drowning. If there is such an answer, he expected it to be found in a brave and lonely quest, not in idle chatter or even in the wisdom of the ages. Those who have listened to the rhythmic crash of the breakers and the wind in the pines and seen the setting sun set the sky on fire across a lake or followed a brook out of a tangled wood can begin to empathize with Robinson's hint at a momentary and very private glimpse of transcendence. In the same poem, he mentions

> . . . those eternal, remote things
> That range across a man's imaginings
> When a sure music fills him and he knows
> What he may say thereafter to few men.[17]

Maine men and women, by and large, tend to agree with Robinson on that score. Whatever their private glimpses, and one suspects there are many, most of them just do not talk about those eternal, remote things very much. And they are embarrassed by those who do. Occasionally, though, as in 1976 when

---

17. Edwin Arlington Robinson, "The Man Against the Sky." Reprinted with permission of Macmillan Publishing Co., Inc. from COLLECTED POEMS by E. A. Robinson. Copyright 1916 by Edwin Arlington Robinson, renewed 1944 by Ruth Nivison.

Benjamin Bubar of Bangor became the most recent in a long line of Maine men to seek the presidency of the United States on the Prohibition ticket, they set out without any embarrassment whatever to reform the world. And like Neal Dow, they are likely to see the world in their image of Maine.

8

Industry, Immigration, and
the Frontier

EIGHTY-FIVE miles up the Penobscot River from Bangor, at the end of a chain of lakes that stretches across half the width of Maine, from Seboomook over near the Quebec border to Pemadumcook Lake and Twin Lakes south of Mount Katahdin, sits Millinocket. Here the sportsman, the backpacker headed for the start of the Appalachian Trail, and the family looking for really primitive camping in Baxter State Park all turn their tailpipes on civilization and begin a narrow, crooked drive into the wilderness.

For the vacationer, then, Millinocket, a jumping-off place perched on the edge of the big woods, serves as a link between civilization and the restoring wilderness. But Millinocket is not there mainly to serve the tourist and the sportsman. It is there to make paper. The sprawling mill buildings beside the West Branch of the Penobscot, the great piles of pulpwood, the sulphur dioxide atmosphere, and the huge rolls of paper stacked aboard flatcars of the Bangor & Aroostook—all these attest to its reason for being.

Millinocket sprang full-blown into being in 1899 and 1900. Where in 1898 there stood only a farm in a clearing, an army of workmen of a half-dozen nationalities created a town that by the fall of 1900 housed 2,000 people and a papermill that was turning out 240 tons of newsprint a day for the Great Northern Paper Company. The building of the "magic city of the North" pretty much rounded out the development of the Maine paper and pulp industry, and it marked the beginning of the shift from co-operative to corporate log-driving on the Penobscot. Beyond that, the overnight creation of a city out of the wilderness to manufacture paper is the best symbol we have of the way Maine went to the Great Barbecue.

The main themes of American history in the years between Reconstruction and World War I—"Gilded Age" industrialization and finance, foreign immigration, and the closing of the frontier—can be studied in microcosm in a single state. Maine had them all (unless you make the plausible argument that here, the frontier is not closed yet), even though students of those themes usually go elsewhere for their material. Entrepreneurs built industries, especially the paper industry, and came to dominate the state's fifteen million acres of forests. Thousands of immigrants came down over the border from Quebec in search of jobs, and in the process created a number of French Canadian enclaves within the larger culture that have continued to add color, diversity, an important work force, and political complexity to Maine life ever since. And the tone and purpose of life on the far northeastern frontier, where thousands of square miles still bear only the numbers of ranges and unorganized townships, mirrored conditions in the far West at the same time.

The entrepreneurial image of exploitation and the immigrant image of opportunity really differed very little from the way the "robber barons" and the European immigrants viewed America at large during the Gilded Age. Predictably, however, and not just because it was smaller, the Maine version had a flavor all its own.

Fish, harbors, trees, and waterpower—in roughly that order of historical sequence—have made up Maine's chief resources from the moment Europeans first started coming there. During the Gilded Age, the Maine fishing business changed sharply with the end of the federal cod bounty in 1868. Maine fishermen on the Grand Banks and all the supporting industries on the

Maine coast that went into the packing of salt cod all but disappeared. Mackerel seining and menhaden catches, which yielded
oil and fertilizer, filled the gap for a time, but then came the discovery of the sardine business about 1875. By the turn of the
century, the Maine sardine, a small herring caught in seines in
the cold inshore waters near Eastport and packed in cans of oil
in sixty-eight factories along the coast, was the nation's second
most important processed fish—next in volume and value only
to canned salmon from Alaska and the Pacific Northwest.

The same era marked the last and possibly most glorious hour
of the Maine sailing ship. William H. Rowe, the maritime historian of Maine, says the magnificent "Down-Easters" that slid
down the ways from Bath to Rockport were alone responsible
for extending the age of the wooden sailing ship a quarter-century beyond the sudden eclipse of the clippers in 1859. Built for
strength and cargo capacity rather than for speed alone, designed originally to carry grain from the Pacific Northwest
around the world, these Maine-built ships commanded by
owners of those stately white houses that line the shaded streets
of towns like Thomaston, Damariscotta, and Searsport carried
the reputation of Maine builders and seamen almost to every
port in the world. And while they lasted—until, that is, they
succumbed to the challenge of the steel-hulled steamship in the
deepwater trade in the late 1890s—they brought handsome
profits to their owners. The great multimasted schooner, also
developed during these same years to carry heavy cargoes with
small crews on the coastwise runs, held on through World War I.

Fish and harbors, therefore, still mattered immensely in these
enterprising years, but it was a new use for trees and waterpower that provoked the new image of massive exploitation.
And it was the characteristics of this new industrial age, combined with some negative circumstances north of the border,
that seemed to offer opportunity to the 38,000 French Canadians
who chose Maine for their new home.

The industrial revolution came to Maine, of course, long
before the post–Civil War takeoff period and eruption of extravagance that Mark Twain christened the "Gilded Age." So, in a
small way, did immigration from Canada. But the tentative

beginning of modern industrialism in the state in the 1830s was really only a spillover from Massachusetts, not an indigenous Maine phenomenon. Railroad development, which spanned the middle third of the century, including the Civil War years, did have some distinctiveness about it with John Poor's unique intercontinental vision, but in early manufacturing, Maine was simply a poor cousin of most of the other New England states. It was, in fact, a Massachusetts combine, the famous Boston Associates, which extended the New England textile industry into Maine by setting up some mills in Biddeford and Saco. These were followed in the 1840s by small mills in several other Maine towns and an important textile concentration in Lewiston. By 1860, Maine had 6,800 of the 81,000 cotton mill workers in New England, ranking fifth in the region; Vermont had practically none. In the same year, Maine had 1,027 of New England's 25,583 woolen mill workers, ranking sixth out of six in New England; and 2,901 of the region's 74,292 workers in the boot and shoe industry, ranking fourth behind Massachusetts, New Hampshire, and Connecticut. Also in the same year, there were living in Maine more than 7,000 French-speaking residents from either Quebec or New Brunswick, about a third of whom had arrived since 1850.

Part of this pre–Civil War immigration had been attracted either by the textile jobs in Biddeford and Saco or by the expanding lumbering opportunities along the lower Penobscot. Most of the immigrants in those years, however, came from the border farming towns of New Brunswick in search of more land just across the Saint John River—where their cousins and compatriots had lived in some numbers since long before the boundary settlement of 1842. So in 1860, two-thirds of the French Canadians in Maine were farmers living away up north at the far end of Aroostook County. This group, by the way, because of its Acadian origins, did not think of itself as *canadien* at all.

The picture changed with the revolution in papermaking soon after 1860, which in turn revolutionized the Maine woodlands and brought a thriving—and smelly—new industry to a dozen Maine towns.

The quest for a substitute for rags as a source of fiber in paper was not new. But it took on new intensity in the middle of the nineteenth century because the demand for paper was growing fast and the supply of rags was not keeping up. Paper, therefore, the medium of the approaching mass culture, the lifeblood of big business and big government, and increasingly the chief ingredient of many manufactured products, was becoming scarce and expensive. In the 1850s, a German scientist invented the first practical method to use wood pulp for the purpose, and the paper revolution was on. By the mid-sixties, papermakers in Pennsylvania and western Massachusetts were going as far as Maine for the poplar trees necessary to feed their pulp mills. The next step was obvious. Overcoming a distorted Middle Atlantic vision of Maine as an endless winter, the paper men began building first pulp mills and then papermills where the wood was. Trees and waterpower—especially along the Androscoggin, the Kennebec, and the Penobscot, which also furnished conduits for floating the pulpwood sticks out of the woods—combined to make Maine one of the nation's leading paper manufacturers within three decades after the owners of a Topsham sawmill began grinding a ton of wood pulp a day in 1868. For Maine, the classic combination of resources was applied this time to the manufacture of a product that helped pull the nation, more quickly than the state, into the commercial and communications worlds of the twentieth century.

Paper- and pulpmills opened in Norway, Mechanic Falls, Canton, Poland, Livermore Falls, Brunswick, Westbrook, Gardiner, and Yarmouth, among other places. Many of these, especially those under the control of Adna C. Denison, the first pulp and paper entrepreneur in Maine, failed as a result either of the depression of 1873–1878 or of overextension and poor business practices in the next decade. The big papermill at Cumberland Mills in Westbrook, however, and subsidiary installations at Gardiner and Yarmouth, were owned by Samuel Dennis Warren, who seems to have understood the paper business better than anyone.

Warren's main plant on a twenty-foot falls on the Presumpscot River was producing paper worth a million dollars a year by 1870. By 1880, after actually raising the level of Sebago

Lake, the source of the river, in order to increase the water-power potential of the falls, the Warren mill was the largest papermill in the world. Warren weathered the depression of the seventies by keeping up steady production and steady employment, but with two pay reductions. Then in 1887, with the coming of better times, he shifted to hydroelectric power and to round-the-clock production by three eight-hour work shifts.

The S. D. Warren Company, under the personal direction of its founder, succeeded because of the right use of machinery and technology and the cultivation of good relations with its employees and the community. Warren paid relatively good wages, led the way with the eight-hour day, encouraged an employees' Mutual Relief Society, lent money to employees, started a profit-sharing plan, and became a benefactor of the town by building a library, financing a church building (which then was named for him), helping the town with public works, erecting 150 company houses that were comfortable and well-equipped for their day, and taking other charitable and essentially paternalistic measures. Far from being resented, however, Warren was rewarded by unusual loyalty in his work force and by the gratitude of the community. One five-day ragsorters' strike in 1880 was Warren's only experience with a labor-caused work stoppage, and his program of community and employee relations virtually forced other Maine papermakers to follow suit and provoked public comment that verged on the adulatory. The *Eastern Argus* of Portland remarked as follows on the Cumberland Mills installation on February 27, 1886:

> Here friction between capital and labor is unknown, affording the best practical example of the true solution to the labor question; and would that it might be more generally followed. Among the other evidences of the good will of the company is a fine popular library to which free access is had every week. Thus do they aim for the mental and moral improvement of the people.[1]

Even as late as the mid-1950s, there were not a few long-time residents of Cumberland Mills who were still gratefully voicing

1. Quoted by David C. Smith in *A History of Lumbering in Maine, 1861–1960*, University of Maine Studies no. 93 (Orono, 1972), p. 241.

the same theme. One of these was an elderly woman whose family's life had always been intertwined with the Warren mill. The S. D. Warren people, she once affirmed thoughtfully in my hearing, "use their help good."

But there was another side to the paper explosion: its effects on the forests. As paper production built up momentum, the demand for pulpwood could no longer be met by putting out annual contracts to nearby farmers to cut a winter's supply of peeled poplar. Technology helped some, because a new pulp process permitted the use of spruce as well as poplar, and the transition to that more plentiful species began in the mid-1880s, though it was not until World War I that spruce virtually replaced poplar as the ingredient of Maine wood pulp. A more fundamental solution was the acquisition of woodlands by the paper companies. Again, it was the S. D. Warren Company that led the way, buying up parcels of forest land near the Sebago–Long Lake waterway and sending pulpwood down the Presumpscot to Cumberland Mills. From 1884 to 1906, these Presumpscot drives, obviously dwarfed by the almost legendary drives of the Kennebec and Penobscot, supplemented contracted pulpwood that arrived by rail from the Fryeburg-Denmark-Brownfield area of Oxford County.

But by the turn of the century, the day of small measures —and small companies—had passed. Just as Rockefeller and Carnegie in oil and steel found the answer to their drive for power and profits in consolidation, so the papermakers of the Northeast got together and made big companies out of little ones, dropping some of the weak ones by the wayside. First came the formation in 1897 of the International Paper Company, owned by a group known as the "giant news combine," which put together the big Androscoggin River mills at Livermore Falls, Rumford, and Berlin, New Hampshire, with almost twenty smaller plants in Maine, Massachusetts, Vermont, and New York. The newest of this group was the mill at Rumford, just recently built in the wilderness at Rumford Falls and destined to become within a few years the center of the industry in Maine. Chief promoter of the Rumford development, which quickly took on an appearance reminiscent of Bangor in its boom days, had been Hugh J. Chisholm of Portland, who now became the first president of International Paper. Before the company was a year old, it was reported to own a million acres of woodland in the United States and 1.6 million acres in Canada. And in his first annual report, President Chisholm announced that the company controlled 90 percent of the production of newsprint in the East.

This was the wave of the future: giant companies, owned by interests in and out of the state—but increasingly outside, because the capital was there—aiming at engrossment of the market, generating their own power through their control of the big rivers, and owning their own supply of their chief raw material. The movement climaxed with the formation of the Great Northern Paper Company and the Northern Development Company, backed almost entirely by New York financiers, which built Millinocket and came to control far more woodland and exercise more impact on the Maine economy than even International Paper, which inspired them.

Firms like S. D. Warren, operating as a community partner within a relatively restricted area, would continue to succeed and attract favorable attention as examples of enlightened and benevolent capitalism. But even such a company found it necessary, with legislative co-operation, to manipulate the level of a large public body of water and engross control of a modest-sized river. And at the same time new giants of the industry, International Paper and the Great Northern, imposed the entrepreneurial spirit of the age, largely with outside capital, upon a waiting state. They overcame with financial and political power whatever resistance stood in the way of their gaining domination of Maine's northern forests and utter control of the big rivers that had been used primarily up to then by co-operative log-driving groups for the benefit of small native woodcutting companies. The transition could not have been more profound. By 1967, even S. D. Warren had capitulated to the consolidating trend and had been absorbed by the Scott Paper Company.

The sharp increase in French-Canadian migration to Maine coincided with the early rise of the paper industry, though not all the new arrivals went to work in papermills. Far from it.

New Brunswick farmers, descendants of the ancient *acadiens,* continued until about 1870 to move across the Saint John to take up farms in Aroostook County, where the border country from Van Buren to Fort Kent is studded with place-names such as Notre Dame, Grand Isle, Frenchville, Guerett, Daigle, and Ouelette. These people, however, were gradually outnumbered after the Civil War by land-poor *canadiens* of Quebec province, equally rural and agricultural in background, who generally followed the Kennebec Valley—Benedict Arnold's route of 1775 in reverse—into central Maine and then went south to the textile mills of Brunswick or Biddeford-Saco or east to the Penobscot, where there were plenty of lumbering jobs near Oldtown and Orono. Some stayed right in the Kennebec Valley, where an important lumbering operation flourished near Skowhegan and Waterville in the 1860s. In the same decade, the first French-Canadian settlers appeared in Lewiston and in Westbrook, destined to become two of the leading French-Canadian centers of Maine. In both cities, the attraction was jobs for unskilled workers in textile mills.

The textile industry was hit by the depression of 1873, and some of the French-Canadian workers who had clustered in several mill towns throughout New England returned to Canada. But the cotton mills of Lewiston held on through the hard times, and in Westbrook the new S. D. Warren Company took up the slack. The coming of the first French-Canadian settlers to the upper Androscoggin towns of Rumford and Livermore Falls coincided exactly with the opening of the papermills there. In this way, certain highly concentrated centers of French-Canadian population had developed by 1900, when Maine residents of French stock numbered 77,000—ten times their number in 1860—in a total population of about 694,000.

Not far from a third of these new Franco-Americans of Maine lived in either the Lewiston-Auburn community, where there were 13,300 of them, or in Biddeford-Saco, where there were 10,650. In Biddeford, French Canadians made up 62 percent of the population, in Brunswick 54 percent, Old Town 52 percent, Lewiston 46 percent, Waterville 45 percent, and in Skowhegan, Sanford, and Westbrook 33 percent or more. Most of them worked in cotton mills. In fact, French Canadians made up 69 percent of the work force in Maine cotton mills in 1900—largely in Biddeford and Lewiston. But they were also well-represented, though in much smaller proportions than in the cotton mills, in Maine brickyards, sawmills, pulp- and papermills, and in the woods as axemen and river drivers.

French Canadians were by no means the only immigrants who arrived in Maine during its industrial takeoff period after the Civil War. Maine has had a sizeable Irish community since early in the nineteenth century. In Lewiston, for example, Irish immigrants were recruited from Boston in the 1830s to build the dam and canal system on the Androscoggin that formed the basis of that city's sprawling textile establishment. By 1850, three-quarters of all the laborers living in Lewiston had been born in Ireland. A recent study by Margaret J. Buker has shown that with few exceptions, the Irish working people who arrived in Lewiston before the great French-Canadian influx of the 1860s did not tend to experience the dramatic increase in wealth and status that one usually associates with the "American dream." [2] Then in the 1870s and 1880s there arrived on a small scale the same general combination of Europeans that thronged to the American Northeast as a whole, with only slight local variations. Swedish immigrants formed one pocket of settlement in Sweden, New Sweden, and Stockholm in the farming country outside of Caribou in northeastern Aroostook County, and another in Piscataquis County south of Moosehead Lake. The newly created paper center of Rumford attracted not only French Canadians in its earliest years, but also immigrants from Norway, Bulgaria, and Poland. Portland acquired a sizeable Italian community in this era, and after World War I and the Russian Revolution and civil war, anti-Bolshevik Russians found their way in some numbers to a few Maine towns. Throughout this period of massive immigration, from about 1870 to a time just after World War I, displaced Jews from the

2. Margaret J. Buker, "The Irish in Lewiston, Maine: A Search for Security on the Urban Frontier, 1850–1880," *Maine Historical Society Quarterly* 13 (special issue 1973): 3–25.

ghettos of central and eastern Europe were among those who looked to the few small urban centers of Maine as a place of opportunity to begin a new life.

By 1920, therefore, Maine had lost the ethnic and religious homogeneity that had perhaps been more myth than reality even from the beginning, but which persists even today as part of the regional stereotype. Perhaps the most supremely ironic paragraphs in all that has ever been written about Maine are the two with which John S. C. Abbott ended his *History of Maine,* published in 1875, just as these various migrations began:

> The flood of foreign immigration is not pouring into Maine as into some other parts of the Union. But this saves the State from a vast amount in inebriation, vagabondage, crime, and pauperism. And those who do select Maine as their home generally come from those countries of Northern Europe where intelligence and piety prevail.
>
> This renders the community in Maine in a remarkable degree homogeneous. The society is in a high degree intelligent, moral, and social. And thus it is that Christian churches arise in every village, that intemperance can be arrested as scarcely anywhere else, that schools and colleges are multiplied, and intelligence and morality are widely diffused. It would be difficult to find in any portion of our land more happy homes than are found in Maine.[3]

Abbott, of course, was wrong on almost every count—except possibly in his last sentence. But to his surprise, no doubt, many of those happy homes by the early twentieth century would house French, Italian, Irish, Scandinavian, and Slavic families as well as Anglo-Saxon ones—not to mention Penobscot and Passamaquoddy families, which did not need to immigrate. The "Christian churches" he spoke of would be Roman Catholic and Eastern Orthodox as well as Protestant, and in a few communities, synagogues and temples would stand beside those. What might have surprised him most of all, if he had searched the evidence that was available even then, was that Father John Baptst, the Jesuit missionary who was serving the French communities in Skowhegan and Waterville in the early

---

3. John S. C. Abbott, *The History of Maine* (Boston: B. B. Russell, 1875), p. 530.

1850s, persuaded his Waterville flock not only to build a mission church but also, in keeping with the principal social concern of the Maine majority in that era, to found a temperance society!

Yes, the immigrants to Maine in the post–Civil War era were almost as diverse a group as the immigrants to the nation at large. Yet in Maine and the rest of New England, the French Canadians remain a special case. They are conspicuous partly because they are by far the largest non-"Yankee" ethnic group, but it is more than that. There is also the language that they retain fiercely, the accented English that is spoken even by the highly educated above middle age, betraying that until recently the language of the larger culture has been for them only a second language, and the special culture that is nourished and perpetuated in churches and parochial schools, a French-language press, and Franco-American protective, fraternal, and cultural societies. Above all, there is their proximity and continual interaction with relatives, friends, and ancestral places and institutions north of the border. In the early years of immigration, in fact, there was a good deal of moving back and forth—and of shifting of places in mills and houses between vacating returnees and new arrivals. European immigrants have come to America bringing their load of cultural baggage with them, but it has not characteristically been a load that has been replenished from abroad once the dilutions and accretions of American life have begun. The normal process, in short, has been assimilation. A public figure like Edmund Muskie, for example, is perceived by the nation as a downeast Yankee, which in fact he is in speech, appearance, and essential values—despite his Polish ancestry, his Catholic religion, and his Democratic politics. A Maine Franco-American, by contrast, rarely regards himself as a "Yankee," nor do his neighbors think of him that way. That does not mean that he is not a loyal and often active citizen. It does mean that his or his father's or his grandfather's move of a few hundred miles across the border has done nothing to change the *quebecois* sense of separateness that has been nourished since 1763 in a bilingual and bicultural society. It has been as natural for the Franco-American to tie his identity to his language and culture, and to assert their validity—even after moving to a country that is not officially bilingual—as it has been for his brother and his cousin a short drive away in Canada to do the same.

Intermarriage, the recent decline of parochial schools, and the staggering increase since World War II in the proportion of young Americans attending college have begun a slow erosion of the vigorous particularity that the French-Canadian community in Maine has retained for a hundred years. For the great majority of Franco-American boys and girls, college has meant the same public universities and private secular or vaguely Protestant colleges that their contemporaries attend. One suspects, however, that not even the next hundred years will be enough to erase the French identity completely. Political activism among Franco-American cousins in Quebec and a resurgence of "ethnicity" among many groups in the United States are alone sufficient to halt any rush toward amalgamation. And the existing monuments to a special French-Canadian culture that now enrich the Maine scene are hardly going to disappear overnight, if indeed they will disappear as long as there is any civilization in Maine at all. These monuments are especially conspicuous in a place like Lewiston, where ice hockey is king, French business signs light the cold sidewalks at night, a magnificent cathedral soars into the sky far above the surrounding tenements, and snowshoe clubs of two nations congregate in brightly colored knee pants and tasseled caps.

On the negative side, the Franco-American's reluctance to climb into the melting pot has made his the most conspicuous important "minority" group in Maine and has therefore contributed to hostility and prejudice from the larger society. Except in the localities he dominates numerically, he has not, with some exceptions, like that of Henri A. Benoit, a leading Portland clothier and proponent of civic development, been brought into the business, political, or cultural life of the state at large. Franco-American politicians in Maine—unlike their counterparts in New Hampshire, Massachusetts, and Rhode Island—still generally seek office only among their own ethnic constituency. They will appear, for example, as mayors of Lewiston, Westbrook, or

Biddeford, but rarely enter congressional or gubernatorial contests. This circumstance, explainable only by the assumption of separateness on both sides, has not yet shown signs of changing. Important appointive posts are not completely closed off, however, as is apparent from the positions held by Chief Justice Armand Dufresne of the Maine Supreme Court and by United States District Court Justice Edward T. Gignoux. On July 4, 1976, the *Maine Sunday Telegram* of Portland published a bicentennial supplement containing the names of some 200 outstanding Maine men and women who had made special contributions to the state and the nation. Only a half-dozen of them—including Judges Dufresne and Gignoux, and also Rudy Vallee, the singer—are identifiably French. In 1896, the *Nation* carried an article on the French Canadians in Maine in which the author observed, "as a class, they are treated considerately in public because of their votes, disparaged in private because of general dislike, and sought by all for the work they do and the money they spend." [4] One cannot help but find lingering evidence of some of the same attitudes eighty years later. But the French Canadians came to Maine and the rest of New England seeking new opportunities for a livelihood without compromising their identity, not for integration. Whatever else may be said, joyous or painful, about this curious subject, most of the Canadian immigrants and most of their descendants can be said with some certainty to have found what they came for.

Industrialization and immigration: two marks of America's Gilded Age replicated by Maine in her own downeast style. The third theme is the frontier. For the Maine version of that, we must look to the eastern part of Aroostook County, a dryer, cooler, flatter country than the rest of Maine, a vast open space that a Presque Isle potato grower predicted in 1858 would be "the garden of the State of Maine." [5]

4. William MacDonald, quoted by Ralph Dominic Vicero in "Immigration of French Canadians to New England, 1840–1900: A Geographic Analysis" (Ph.D. diss., University of Wisconsin, 1968), p. 367.
5. Quoted by Clarence A. Day in *Farming in Maine, 1860–1940,* University of Maine Studies no. 78 (Orono, 1963), p. 129.

The farmer, George F. Whidden, told the secretary of the Maine Board of Agriculture that the only thing lacking for the realization of that dream was a railroad to Bangor. He had caught some of the enthusiasm of John Poor, who at that moment was at the peak of his influence and accomplishment in Portland. By 1878, Fort Fairfield and Caribou had rail connections with the outside world by way of the New Brunswick & Canada and the European & North American, and in 1894 the Bangor & Aroostook finally provided the long-awaited direct line from Caribou, Fort Fairfield, and Houlton to Bangor. The rail links gave the Aroostook farmers an outlet for their potatoes, which swiftly became—and remain—Maine's leading cash crop.

Settlers from the lower parts of Maine had begun taking up land in the county in some numbers after the Webster-Ashburton Treaty settled the boundary with New Brunswick in 1842. Dr. Ezekiel Holmes, the father of scientific farming in Maine, had visited the region in 1838 and written a good report on the land's growing potential, especially for potatoes. To encourage settlement, the state sold land for fifty cents an acre, but only to actual settlers, and allowed the buyers to earn most of the purchase price by working on the roads.

By 1860, 22,000 people lived in Aroostook, and by 1870 there were more than 3,000 farms and 133,000 acres of improved land. These earliest settlers did not concentrate solely on potatoes as their successors did. Potatoes were too bulky to ship by wagon over the muddy "Military Road" to Bangor. Wheat, oats, buckwheat, and grass seed were the favored exports during the prerailroad years. Meanwhile, the farmers could sell grain, hay, and potatoes to lumbermen working the Saint John River.

The railroad connections of 1878 prompted the immediate shipment of potatoes, and by 1880, twenty starch mills were turning a large part of the crop into a more easily exportable and highly marketable commodity. Starch accounts even today for a part of the Aroostook potato crop, but seed potatoes and eating potatoes are more important than they were once, and local processed food plants now form a good part of the outlet by manufacturing things like frozen French fries. The opening of the Bangor & Aroostook produced even more dramatic effects than the earlier rail connection. In the 1890s, potato acreage jumped from 16,600 almost to 42,000 acres and in the next decade nearly to 76,000 acres. With increasing success in growing and marketing potatoes, even with occasional bad years, the farmers of Aroostook turned more and more toward an economy based on the one staple crop. Early efforts by staff members of the state Board of Agriculture and other experts failed to interest farmers in growing sugar beets. In the 1960s, however, efforts at diversification seemed finally to be paying off, in the face of huge potato harvests not only in Aroostook but elsewhere in the nation, and also because of changes in the national diet resulting in smaller potato consumption and consequent declining potato prices. Sugar beets, processed in a local sugar refinery, were becoming the main alternate crop. But neither the Aroostook soil nor the climate is ideal for sugar beets, and the alternate crop does not hold brilliant promise. The refinery was forced to close for a time. It is now open again, but the future of the Maine sugar beet industry is not yet really assured.

With the help of a generous state land policy, the Maine Agricultural Experiment Station, the University of Maine, the Extension Service, the United States Department of Agriculture, and the Bangor & Aroostook Railroad, pioneering farmers actually set Aroostook to blooming during the Gilded Age and beyond. Maine politicians and visitors alike often noticed a "Western spirit of enterprise" [6] in this sparsely settled region. Even in modern times, one notices the proliferation of Cadillacs and the newest equipment and the sprucing up of buildings and grounds right after the harvest in a good potato year. Life and speech alike are a bit more expansive than they are to the southward and eyes are still on acres left to till. Yet the Aroostook farmer, businessman and opportunist though he may be, is no Texan. If there is a "frontier mind" here at all, it is a mature and subdued one. In Aroostook, the good years are taken advantage of, but always with the consciousness that a local blight or a big national crop can put the whole county in the hole. When

6. Day, *Farming in Maine,* p. 134.

that happens, the people of Aroostook weather the storm philo-
sophically and wait for a good season to recoup their losses. So
there is an expansiveness and a hospitality and an orientation
toward the future that is without extravagance and without vul-
garity. An Aroostook farmer, "frontier" and all, is still a Yankee.

Industrialization, immigration, the frontier. Maine had a special version of all of them during the nation's Gilded Age.
These produced in turn two more images of Maine: a place of
opportunity, and a place of exploitation. During the same
period, again as part of a tendency operating elsewhere in the
nation as well, it acquired still another image. It became a place
of retreat.

9

Natives and Strangers

$\mathcal{T}$HE stories are legion.

A lean, leather-brown figure in a khaki shirt and baseball cap pumps gas into a Massachusetts tank outside the general store of one of those peninsular hamlets somewhere between South Harpswell and Bucks Harbor. "Sure are some funny people around here," the owner of the car offers by way of friendly if not overly diplomatic conversation. "Ayuh," the native inhales agreeably, then pauses—for in this sort of exchange, timing is everything. "But," he adds finally, "most of 'em be gone by Labuh Day."

Or an out-of-stater braces himself on the open deck of a pitching fishing boat steering out of a harbor despite threatening weather. He looks up and is encouraged. "It seems to be clearing overhead," he observes hopefully to the skipper. "Yup," the salty one agrees. Maine pause. "But that ain't where we're headed." [1]

I remember an occasion long ago when not even the Maine registration plates on my aged Ford earned me more than a lone monosyllable. Was this the way to Sebasco, I wanted to know of a whiskered pipe-smoker rocking on a front porch overlook-

---

1. These are hearsay versions of anecdotes that probably first showed up in print in the bible of the coasting sailor, Roger F. Duncan's and Fessenden S. Blanchard's *Cruising Guide to the New England Coast*. For the pristine versions, see the 5th ed. rev. (New York: Dodd, Mead, 1965), pp. 261, 354–355.

ing the gravel road. "Nope." The puffing and the rocking continued without missing a beat. The Maine pause was a long one,
so long in fact that eventually it became obvious that the sage
considered the question fairly answered, as I suppose it was. I
drove off and eventually reached my destination with no more
trouble than I have suffered occasionally from garrulous
direction-givers who try to be more helpful than they need to
be.

The point in all these anecdotes is more complicated than
might appear. They illustrate the famous Maine taciturnity,
especially the last. But not all Mainers are taciturn, despite
legend. In addition, the stories convey a little of the official
Maine sense of humor, which loves the quiet ironic twist, the
turning of the table. More important, though, they all have to do
with the curious relationship between natives and strangers in
the state that proclaims itself "Vacationland."

Tourism is Maine's most important industry. Today you can
find plenty of innkeepers and motel operators, landlords, gift
shop operators, and bartenders and waitresses who not only accept that reality but enjoy it. These are the Maine people who
are likely to have grown up after World War II, traveled and
gone to college, and adopted, either in self-defense or because
they find some positive fulfillment there, the "other-
directedness" and outgoing personality of the salesman. You
may not be able to tell from their accent whether their roots in
Maine are deep or whether they are really outlanders come to
enjoy the air and the relative simplicity of Maine life and live
off the tourist trade. You will even find some who run a motel
in Maine in summer and then go to Florida to do the same thing
in winter. Whether newcomers or homogenized sons and daughters of natives, this type, like its counterpart everywhere else,
bends backwards to be kind, charming, and persuasive, often
using nondescript speech in the process. No dour, abbreviated,
half-amused, sharp-tongued country back talk from them!

Fortunately for the regional backbone, however, there are still
some authentic voices to be heard in the areas visited by tourists
and part-time residents. The farther east you go, the more likely
you are to hear them. These are not necessarily unfriendly

voices, but there is no false face on them. From them it is possible to learn that dependence upon serving visitors for part of one's livelihood need not mean either deference or sullen resentment. Nor need it involve a surrender of individuality or a compromise of personal integrity.

The question remains why any segment of the Maine people, even a minority, should cling so fiercely to its identity, which includes a certain cautious scrutiny when it comes to dealing with strangers. For a few, undoubtedly, there is simply the shrewd guess that this kind of local color is what the visitor expects when he comes to Maine, and the more of it he gets the longer he may stay and the more money he may spend.

But there are far more who do not play at being "characters." For them, the answer is more complex, and it can only be a guess. It may seem strange to go to Dixie for a parallel, but there are comparisons that can be made, however distasteful it may be to both sides, between northern New England and the Deep South. In the rural areas of both, provincialism of speech, dress, and manner hangs on more stubbornly than in most parts of the nation. Both regions possess a past glory that neither the present nor the future now appears likely to match. Both are poorer than the nation at large, and both depend upon economies larger than their own, controlled from outside their regions, for their survival. The Southland has lived for more than a century with the painful consciousness of defeat in war and the passing of a distinctive way of life which, however rooted in evil most southerners acknowledge it to have been, was the definitive mark of their region. The most sensitive southerners have accepted the defeat and the passing with dignity and introspection, admitting the reality and even the evil while holding on to what remains of the culture and the code and above all to the sense of place, all of which give meaning to their existence as a distinct people. In a perverse but profoundly moving way, as any reader of William Faulkner knows, these elements of southernness have been enriched and sanctified by tragedy.

The tragedies of Maine and the rest of northern New England have been mostly economic and demographic rather than moral and military. Perhaps that is why the defense mechanisms that respond to them are less militant, more quietly humorous, than those that respond to the tragedies of the South.

Maine farmers had started "moving out" about 1830, about the time the sheep craze died, because it was obvious that the new rail connections with eastern markets would make the vast open, easily tillable lands of the Midwest a more profitable place to farm than the hilly rocky soil of New England. The exodus, real as it was, was not attracting great attention in the pre–Civil War years because most eyes, with John Poor's, were fixed on the future. But by 1860, some 50,000 natives of Maine were living outside New England. About half of those were in the farm country of the Midwest, about 6,000 were toiling on the new timber frontier of Minnesota, and about 10,000 were in California, where Maine ships had been calling for two generations and where New Englanders flocked after the gold strike of 1849. Most of the rest were farming in Pennsylvania or New York State. The rate of increase in Maine's population declined as soon as the "moving out" began. Yankee farmers and woodsmen moved out far faster than French-Canadian and European immigrants replaced them. Natural increase kept the population growing, but much more slowly than before.

By 1900 at the latest, the Maine folk who still lived on farms south of Aroostook or made their living from the sea were conscious that time had somehow passed them by. The textile and paper industries were in a different world from theirs, and in any case were not enough to maintain the relative position in the Union in population and wealth with which Maine had begun her life as a state and which had been declining almost ever since. Dominance in shipbuilding and ocean trade, it was now obvious, had been tied to the proximity and overwhelming abundance of timber and also resulted from generations of highly developed, transmitted skills in building wooden hulls and handling sailing ships at sea. With the revolution in technology, neither of these factors remained paramount, and the maritime centers moved elsewhere; Bath alone adapted to steel and steam on an important scale and single-handedly maintained as best she could the maritime contributions of the state. In in-

dustry and most other fields, Maine sat just too far to the northeast, too far out on the edge of the national transportation networks developed during the Gilded Age. These networks tie
together the raw materials, food, labor, science, management,
sellers, and markets that combine to make the complex, integrated national industrial-commercial network of the twentieth
century. If prosperity, population, and national influence were
the measures by which a state ought to fix a value upon its identity, then clearly Maine was fast becoming more interesting and
valuable for its past than for its future. Like the postbellum
South.

And it was just then that the summer people began to come.
This was not the touring crowd, or the family camping set of a
later day, nor was it primarily the romantic rustic, coming as
Thoreau had come in the 1840s to read the book of nature. The
first summer visitors of modern times came to Maine precisely
to enjoy that past. Not that they knew or cared much about history, most of them, but they were aware that away to the northeast of Boston, neither the beauties of nature nor the pace of life
had yet been spoiled by the sudden industrialization and ur-
banization that were now transforming their home cities of Boston, New York, and Philadelphia. So they came to enjoy a past
that they had traded away at home for horizontal and vertical integration, interlocking directorates, and all the smoke, steam,
coal, oil, steel, and wealth that went with them.

And when they came in summer to York Harbor, Ogunquit,
Kennebunkport, Boothbay, Isleborough, Camden, and Bar Harbor, they brought their money with them. They built lavish
"cottages" and learned to sail yachts, depending upon simple
farmers and fishermen, whom they pronounced "quaint," and
perhaps here and there the proud scion of a sadly diminished
seafaring or shipbuilding family, to build and maintain their
property and teach them the practical ways of the shore and the
sea. True, many of the people of Boothbay and Bar Harbor
became dependent, in turn, upon the summer cottagers for much
of their livelihood. But as for "society," the visitors made their
own, associating only with each other in "reading rooms,"
yacht clubs, and each other's dining rooms, and on tennis

courts, horse tracks, and, after a time, golf courses. Thus the beneficiaries of the economic revolution of the 1870s, 1880s, and 1890s exported the Gilded Age to Maine on their own terms, as they did at the same time to Newport.

Professional and business families of more modest means now began coming by train to spend genteel summers rocking on piazzas and playing croquet and tennis at quiet, correct resort hotels whose high-ceilinged lobbies were swept by lake or ocean breezes. My grandmother was one of a small group of prim young Boston schoolteachers who, near the turn of the century, discovered the delights of spending some of the warm weeks on a saltwater farm near the Kennebec. The farmer's two youngest sons took upon themselves the special duty of making visitors like this feel at home. The eventual result was two weddings, all very romantic and proper, and the Boston girls moved to Maine, became good farmers' wives, and soon began to take in summer guests themselves.

In time, of course, as the wealth of the new civilization filtered down to the middle class in the form of family automobiles and paid vacations, there occurred a democratization of the Maine summer. By the 1920s, caravans of tourists on gradually improving roads were supplementing the quieter enclaves of the rich in their summer colonies, and Maine folk were learning that there was money to be made from them. Owners of gracious houses in the villages along coastal U.S. Route 1 and Scenic 1A put in electric lights and flush toilets and put out illuminated signs welcoming overnight paying guests. Tourist cabins, each cozily accommodating two travelers in a double bed, appeared in little clusters grouped along a driveway or around a court or perhaps secluded romantically on the edge of a pine grove. Each little village of eight or a dozen cabins had a name like "Maine Idyll" or "Half Moon" painted on a huge sign beside the white center-lined concrete of U.S. 1. And out-of-state fishermen discovered Sebago and the Rangeleys and Moosehead, and in November carloads of red-jacketed good fellows drove up into the big woods, stopping at L. L. Bean's in Freeport, open twenty-four hours a day, for ammunition and perhaps a pair of Bean's famous leather-topped, rubber-bottomed hunting boots. They drove home, the lucky ones, with their deer trussed on their front fenders and a week's growth of he-man's beard.

The beaches at York, Wells, Ocean Park, and Old Orchard (but not Ogunquit, the best of all, which came instead under the early influence of wealthy summer colonists and a cluster of artists) sprouted modest, closely packed cottages. The cottage colony at Ocean Park, a part of Old Orchard, developed around a camp meeting ground set up in a grove in 1873, and gradually acquired additional facilities for religious conferences; Old Orchard proper, by strange contrast, grew into a vast amusement park, visited by great numbers of Canadian as well as New England tourists, where by 1976 the townspeople were voting in a special referendum that the "topless" waitresses in the Bikini Tavern must cover their pretty bosoms. And highway bridges spanned the Piscataqua and the Kennebec so that middle-class families in touring cars could drive easily from Newton and Braintree and even Worcester and Hartford to the beaches with their cottages or farther Down East to the little villages on the peninsulas with their lobster pounds and their little inns and their gift shops. And some enterprising Yankee advertised a little natural freak and called it the Desert of Maine and brought in a camel, and the tourists went to see that, too.

After World War II, when the Maine Turnpike bypassed U.S. 1 to take station wagons and camping vans from New Jersey and Ohio down east at seventy miles an hour, some of the tourists speeding for the first time through this part of their endless itinerary came to expect "attractions" prepared for their consumption. "What is there to take in here?" a carload of New Yorkers in effect demanded of a friend of mine whose appreciation of the Wiscasset-Damariscotta-Pemaquid region is so deep-rooted and emotional that it is almost tangible. His response tried to convey the notion that there was nothing here at all that could with any satisfaction be "taken in" and checked off as "done." Visitors like these lack the time for the necessary exploration and the necessary savoring. Maine, despite the mutations brought by a hundred years of tourism, remains Maine; it does not even yet show signs of becoming Dis-

neyland, despite a few shabby attempts along the highways to
make it that. But the image of Maine as vacationland and nothing else is a persistent one in our day. A little Massachusetts girl
one of my students knows, informed that one of the people con-
versing with her lived in Maine the year round, responded:
"But you can't be from Maine. Maine's closed in the winter."

Clearly, the folks who live in Maine and love their place and
way of life are aware of the tragedy in all this. Some have
responded less than nobly, either with a hopeless shrug at the
inevitability of decline and poverty or with shamefully ob-
sequious attempts to court the stranger—or what is just as destructive, resentment of him. But for those who have reflected
more deeply on the meaning of the last hundred years, the
response to a kind of tragedy has been more fulfilling. In the
poem "New Hampshire," Robert Frost wrote, "No state can
build/A literature that shall at once be sound/And sad on a foundation of well-being." [2]

Well, Maine has built a literature and an art, and a saving
remnant of her ordinary citizens has made an art out of life and
character. Sarah Orne Jewett, who some say is Maine's finest
writer, had this to say about a small flowering shrub that does
not grow out of "a foundation of well-being":

> Who can laugh at my Marsh Rosemary, or who can cry, for that
> matter? The gay primness of the plant is made up from a hundred
> colors if you look close enough to find them. This Marsh Rosemary
> stands in her own place, and holds her dry leaves and tiny blossoms
> steadily toward the same sun that the pink lotus blooms for, and the
> white rose. [3]

There Miss Jewett blurted out how she felt about quiet beauty
that stands erect, proudly but unpretentiously, being its sturdy,

2. From "New Hampshire" from THE POETRY OF ROBERT FROST, edited by
Edward Connery Lathem. Copyright 1923, © 1969 by Holt, Rinehart and Winston.
Copyright 1951 by Robert Frost. Reprinted by permission of Holt, Rinehart and Win-
ston, Publishers.

3. Sarah Orne Jewett, "Marsh Rosemary," quoted by Willa Cather in Preface to
Jewett, *The Country of the Pointed Firs and Other Stories* (Garden City, N.Y.: Double-
day & Co., 1956), p. 8.

steady self amidst surrounding splash and glitter. She might have been thinking of her own art, as Willa Cather has suggested, growing in a new country "out of a thin new soil." [4] But in late nineteenth-century America, blustering and bullying and ballyhooing its way into extravagance in business and consumption at home and doubtful adventures abroad, the Marsh Rosemary might as easily have been the authentic people of Maine, doomed and privileged to stand steadily in their own place, watching with gay primness the passing parade of pink lotuses and white roses on their way to Bar Harbor.

With lovely, sad descriptive passages blending natural landscape, the humblest works of man, and human character, Miss Jewett knew how to tell the truth about the hard and lonely life of the fishermen's coast. For example:

> These ancient seafarers had houses and lands not outwardly different from other Dunnet Landing dwellings, and two of them were fathers of families, but their true dwelling places were the sea, and the stony beach that edged its familiar shore, and the fishhouses, where much salt brine from the mackerel kits had soaked the very timbers into a state of brown permanence and petrifaction. It also affected the old fishermen's hard complexions, until one fancied that when Death claimed them it could only be with the aid, not of any slender modern dart, but the good serviceable harpoon of a seventeenth century woodcut. [5]

And from another portion of *The Country of the Pointed Firs,* her classic long story of 1896:

> The coast had still a wintry look; it was far on in May, but all the shore looked cold and sterile. One was conscious of going north as well as east, and as the day went on the sea grew colder, and all the warmer air and bracing strength and stimulus of the autumn weather, and storage of the heat of summer, were quite gone. I was very cold and very tired when I came at evening up the lower bay, and saw the white houses of Dunnet Landing climbing the hill. They had a friendly look, these little houses, not as if they were climbing up the shore, but as if they were rather all coming down to

---

4. Preface to Jewett, *Country of the Pointed Firs,* p. 8.
5. Jewett, *Country of the Pointed Firs,* p. 102.

meet a fond and weary traveler, and I could hardly wait with patience to step off the boat.[6]

Here is how one writer, daughter of a Maine country doctor, responded to her place with authenticity and integrity in the midst of change—by telling truths about it which were at once hard and beautiful. Miss Jewett hardly began the fashion of writing fiction with a Maine setting; she, in fact, had been inspired by Harriet Beecher Stowe's *Pearl of Orr's Island,* which had followed *Uncle Tom's Cabin* by eleven years, and Sally Sayward Barrel Wood of York had written pioneering, Maine-based fiction half a century before that. But besides her own contributions to a literature that was regional without being provincial and quaint, Miss Jewett set in motion an outpouring of books by influencing Mary Ellen Chase, who was born in Blue Hill in 1887 and went to the University of Maine, and Gladys Hasty Carroll of Miss Jewett's own South Berwick, who went to Bates. In roughly the generation of these latter two—born between 1885 and 1900 and writing mainly during the first half of the twentieth century—have been the poets Edna St. Vincent Millay and Robert Peter Tristram Coffin and the historical novelist Kenneth Roberts, all writers with sturdy Maine roots who used Maine settings and Maine characters to produce literature with universal themes. Edwin Arlington Robinson, born in 1869, came earlier—and wrote critically of his place, as when he described "Old Eben Flood," the drunk of Tilbury Town (which no doubt was Gardiner) and speaks of the joyless, loveless qualities of those who live "Here where the wind is always north-north-east/And children learn to walk on frozen toes." [7]

And the visual arts also began to flourish, especially in oils and watercolors. Winslow Homer, Fitz Hugh Lane, John Marin, and Marsden Hartley captured through various eyes the perma-

6. Jewett, *Country of the Pointed Firs,* p. 147.
7. "Old Eben Flood" and "New England," by Edwin Arlington Robinson in *Collected Poems* (New York: Macmillan Co., 1937), pp. 573–575, 900–901. Quotation reprinted with permission of Macmillan Publishing Co., Inc. from COLLECTED POEMS by Edwin Arlington Robinson. Copyright 1925 by Edwin Arlington Robinson, renewed 1953 by Ruth Nivison and Barbara R. Holt.

nent realities that they found in the powerful interactions of natural forms, and Andrew Wyeth conveyed in watercolors a nostalgic vision of a lovely place not far removed from Miss Jewett's word-pictures of several decades before.

The intellectual and artistic response to the decline of the Maine economy, the moving out, and the coming of the summer people, then, was the assertion of the dignity, the beauty, and the integrity of the place and its people. There was something about Maine, they said, that had a worth of its own that did not depend upon imposed standards or imported money. Part of that assertion lay in the fresh discovery of its breathtaking natural beauty. Another part lay in a fresh appreciation of a certain kind of human character.

Seba Smith had discovered the regional character with Jack Downing half a century before Miss Jewett came on the scene. Downing, of course, was an amusing caricature, as are the conversations in the currently popular "Bert and I" record series sold by *Down East* magazine. The important thing about him, though, is that he was intended to be laughed at, not only by outsiders, but also by his own kind—as are "Bert and I." The regional self-consciousness before Jack Downing often manifested itself in humor directed at outsiders. To the extent that Mainers have resorted to a pre–Jack Downing put-down of strangers as a defense against an inferiority complex, there has been a dreadful reversion. Fortunately, however, expressions of out-and-out resentment and hostility, from what I have seen, are rare. The regional assertions of the best literature and art, whether funny or serious, seek out and illuminate the values inherent in Maine, often appreciatively and sometimes critically, but never apologetically and never at the expense of others. Invidiousness would spoil the whole point of independent self-worth, and turn a dignified regional consciousness into a narrow provincialism.

So it is with the true Maine Yankees. Louise Dickinson Rich, who has written several charming books about Maine, settled down years ago way Down East at Prospect Harbor, which is in Corea, a tiny lobstering town on Gouldsborough Peninsula not far from Schoodic Point. Of the natives, she writes. "I like the way they treat me, as though I were a reasonably sane human being." [8] It may be that Mrs. Rich, with her immense store of Maine coastal lore, has a greater claim to respect than most outlanders. But my own experiences as a continually returning native, and the experiences of friends of mine whose connections with Maine are far more sporadic and casual than that, all suggest that visitors who deserve to be treated as reasonably sane human beings will be treated that way. There is pride and self-assurance and not a little shrewdness among the natives who deal with strangers, but rarely any meanness. On the contrary, there is sincere helpfulness and genuine friendliness, not effusive or overdrawn but practical and solid. Maine villagers and country dwellers are accustomed to "helping out" one another a good deal when the occasion demands, and assume that that is part of ordinary human relations, no matter who is involved. They will go out of their way when necessary, therefore, to rescue a stalled car or boat, give gardening or fishing advice, locate some firewood, recommend handymen, or discourse on the price of lobster or some received version of local history. The image of Maine taciturnity is badly distorted; it is only idle, pointless chatter that is spurned.

The pride in Maine identity is expressed everywhere, and in ways that are sometimes surprising. Nowhere in the eastern United States, for example, are you likely to find more state flags fluttering from home flagpoles. One car owner of New Harbor on Pemaquid peninsula announces both his place and his native tongue by arranging the letters on his "vanity" license plate to spell NUHABA. Homeowners throughout the state love to use the pine tree motif on shutters, weathervanes, garage gables, and the like, and those near the coast often add the gull and work a few bright lobster buoys into the decor. A series of advertising billboards appropriates the multisyllabic Maine affirmative "ayuh." As early as 1972, when the study of state and local history was just beginning to reacquire academic respect-

---

8. Louise Dickinson Rich, *The Coast of Maine: An Informal History and Guide* (New York: Thomas Y. Crowell, Co., 1975), p. 340.

ability, professional students of Maine history in the state organized themselves into a group called the Maine Academic Historians, which operates in association with the Maine Historical
Society. They discovered the following year that Maine residents could choose among no fewer than six serious academic
courses in the University of Maine system and elsewhere to
study the history of their state.

And the typical Maine Yankees, even if they can afford it, do
not go far afield for their own vacations. They do not really go
away on vaction anyway, unless they go to Florida in winter,
but if occupation and finances permit this kind of self-
indulgence, they are likely to spend the summer not more than
an hour's drive away from home in "camp," a highly informal
place on some water somewhere, which if not built with the
owner's own hands was doubtless inherited from someone who
did build it that way. I have not taken exact count lately, but I
daresay that of the twenty or thirty "camps" along a mile or so
of Sebago Lake shoreline that I have known for some thirty-five
years, at least three-quarters of them are occupied most of every
summer by owners who can drive from there to their year-round
homes or to their work in a half-hour. Many Portlanders have
summer places on the islands of Casco Bay. Maine families
who go tenting or hiking are likely to keep a good share of their
expeditions within their own state, the expanse and natural variety of which many Mainers feel a conscious compulsion to
explore and know better. The same is true of Maine coastal
sailors. Conversely, outside a place like Portsmouth, New
Hampshire, which serves as a shopping center for a small part
of southwestern Maine and for the navy yard in Kittery, Maine
automobiles are a rarity in the five other New England states,
almost as much as cars from Vermont, which has only half the
people that Maine has. In fact, my own highly unscientific survey of highway traffic in the six New England states over the
past thirty years yields the following results: that Maine, with
the third-largest population in New England and the greatest variety of out-of-state and even out-of-country cars on its own
highways, is fifth in the likelihood that one of its drivers will be

found beyond his own state boundary. The point, of course, is that Maine people are proud of their state; one way they express that pride is by staying there most of the time.

Maine Yankees, those who carry pride in place and self with dignity, match their self-respect with a respect, even an admiration, for certain qualities in others. An elderly janitor in my college dormitory who came in to work every day from somewhere in the Maine countryside never hesitated to drop a caustic complaint over the disgraceful state in which my roommates and I kept our room, or to moralize over the evidences of mild dissipation that were here and there apparent in the dormitory. One morning, however, I glanced up from typing a term paper to see him leaning in the doorway, just looking. "Nothing I like better," he explained without apology, "than watching a man who knows what he's doing." Now I confess that I would have preferred praise from a man of his values and standards for doing something a bit more strenuous and substantial, but the remark was offered with utter sincerity and goodwill. And I think it reflected a characteristic Maine attitude: an appreciation of diligence and craftsmanship, no matter how alien the activity. Maine people also, despite their almost legendary sharpness in a deal, admire honesty in others and despise fakery.

Margaret Chase Smith reflected this quality as spokesman for the seven Republican United States senators who in June 1950 issued the famous "Declaration of Conscience" against the tactics of fellow Republican Joseph R. McCarthy. Mrs. Smith, the only woman in the Senate, said McCarthy's accusatory, Red-hunting tactics were aimed at "riding the Republican party to victory through the selfish political exploitation of fear, bigotry, ignorance, and intolerance." [9] Neither she nor her six colleagues, including two from neighboring New Hampshire and Vermont, would stand for it. This was a courageous act in that difficult era, but it was in keeping with this most admirable of regional traditions.

Maine people respond in kind to friendly conversation, drawing the line only if the interrogation gets personal; in return,

9. *New York Times,* June 2, 1950, pp. 1, 11.

they resist prying into the private affairs of strangers, at least to their faces. And they admire, to be frank, material success. What they do not admire are the airs that often go with it—and you will find a few natives who have turned some ancestral coastal land into a gold mine of well-managed summer property but who differ not a bit from their less-fortunate neighbors in conversation, clothing, manners, neighborliness, or daily routine. In short, they remain themselves. And they respect those, natives or strangers, who do the same.

The native residents' image of Maine since the tourist revolution has been an image of home, a home that they sense has become diminished in economic and political importance but to which, out of that very consciousness, they have developed a fierce attachment. The land to which they belong fosters a sense of permanence, as does the study of local history and genealogy in which someone in their families will almost invariably be engaged. For many Maine people, the tourist revolution has sharpened their vision of the natural beauty they once took for granted, a beauty that has also helped to generate a pride in place along with the practical awareness of the necessity of marketing the place to others. And the Mainers' image of place includes a vision of self, a recognizable regional character, distinct from similar types elsewhere. At worst, this character can be provincial, ignorant, and surly with outsiders. At best, it is open and simple, rejecting sham and pretense, recognizing its inseparableness from family and locality and the landscapes and occupations which have helped to shape it, proud of its integrity and its tartness and its humor, and true to itself while tolerant of the strangers upon whom the state's economy largely depends.

There are, however, other images of Maine in the era of the tourist trade. For some, it is a place of escape from a world of haste and crowds and pollution, a world that increasingly presses in. To drive up the New Hampshire Turnpike and soar across the high new Piscataqua River bridge to Maine is to experience freedom. At least it is when the traffic is not bumper-to-bumper, and even at those dismal times, there is the certainty of almost unlimited elbow room some distance to the north or east, never more than an hour or two beyond Kittery. For these and others, it is also a place of refreshment. Mountain and forest wilderness, fishing and canoeing streams, hiking trails, clear lakes, a thousand lovely offshore islands, ski slopes and winter crosscountry trails, and the eternally moving sea against hard-packed beaches and the ragged ledges that guard the edge of Maine—all these nourish the soul, the mind, and the body, and equip a person better to confront what he commonly regards as the "real" world again after his brief retreat. Then there are the consumers of curiosity and entertainment, certain that a state that advertises itself as "vacationland" has natural curiosities and man-made delights ready for them to sample and buy. On another level, Maine is for many of its visitors a source of instruction. Its rich past is documented by monuments, restorations, preservations, and archaeological digs. The magnificent architecture of its seacoast, especially of the early nineteenth century, is well preserved and constitutes a vast and valuable museum. Its villages and countryside provide insights into ways of life that in more populous areas vanished with the modern era. And at Acadia National Park, founded in 1916 on and about Mount Desert Island, and at dozens of other sites less institutionalized, including especially Monhegan Island, the student of nature finds gardens of plenty.

Beyond these uses by the casual visitor, all of which involve a similar image despite their variety in seriousness and worthiness, there is another image of "home" that rivals the native residents' in intensity. The broad westward scattering of the people of Maine in the nineteenth century was reinforced by a similar movement in the twentieth. Economic opportunities elsewhere continued to attract young Maine men and women during the first half of the century, and then after World War II mobility became a way of life for a whole generation of Americans. To work for the government or for a national corporation or to enter academic or professional life meant the certainty of moving about. If a person from Maine worked into one of these positions through the new opportunity for education, the odds were great that the move was made out of the state, given the geographic distribution of jobs of this kind. Thus there were many young Maine families who joined the wandering throng of the fifties and sixties, but somehow the rootlessness and geographic neutrality that characterizes the group in general does not seem to have spread to those with Maine origins. Or at least so another highly unscientific survey of mine suggests. No doubt there are other places—certainly it is true of most of New England—that tug insistently on the sensibilities of wandering sons and daughters, but none tugs more strongly, I think, than Maine.

One need not, apparently, be a native to feel the pull. For there are children and even grandchildren of those nineteenth-century emigrants who have come "Back East," searching out ancestral graveyards and cellar holes, sniffing the surf and the mud flats, contemplating overgrown and useless orchards and forested former sheep pastures, and consulting genealogical dictionaries in the Maine Historical Society. Some of them stay, either seasonably or year-round. And who can deny them the right to call this home? Likewise, I suspect, there lurks in the hearts of many of the more recent emigrants a conviction that for all the comfort and prosperity that their wandering lives may have brought them, it is the natural grandeur and human simplicity of Maine that remains the most likely source of whatever sense of permanence and rootedness they may yearn for. For these, too, Maine is home.

10

The Images Clash

$\mathcal{T}$OURISM has brought thousands of visitors from the outside world into contact with the Maine Yankee, who has responded by cultivating an integrity of character while serving the tourist and seasonal resident for profit. But Maine also has plenty of natives whom the tourists rarely see, and who do not depend upon the tourist trade for their livelihood. They work in the woods or struggle on marginal farms or harvest blueberries or work in mills and factories or provide services for their neighbors. By far the majority live in modest circumstances; more than ought to be are plain poor. Personal income in Maine averaged $4,439 in 1974, sixth in New England and forty-third in the nation, almost $1,000 below the national average and $1,250 below the New England average.[1]

The considerable number of Maine's 994,000 people who live a scraping, struggling, unlovely though usually proud existence are not to be found, typically, in the picture-book villages that dot the coastline, but in the mill towns and in the least dramatic parts of the backcountry. This is the Maine that artists do not paint, writers do not usually describe, and visitors do not talk much about. It is the Maine where scrubby woodlands alternate with bleak, unshaded villages marked by an old general

---

1. U.S. Bureau of Census, *Statistical Abstracts of the United States: 1975,* 96th ed., (Washington, D. C.: Bureau of Census, 1975), p. 388.

store and a Baptist church, but also by a laundromat, a couple of gas stations, and a Dairy Joy, and where the houses may have sheet-metal roofs. It is the Maine where the "mobile home," often embellished with extras and supplemented by an unfinished garage, has replaced the tar-paper shack of thirty years ago in the new clearing beside the road. Here there are junked cars, sawmills, piles of slabwood, spring mud, cornfields, rusty farm equipment, leaning silos, gravel pits, and everlastingly burning town dumps—visited in many cases by what at first seems a shockingly paradoxical scavenger, the seagull. And just to make the general impression of shabbiness more stark, the landscape is punctuated every so often by a well-fenced farm with a nicely painted stand of buildings, a big cornfield or potato field, lovely meadows for haying, and a herd of purebred dairy cattle grazing in an expansive pasture with a water hole—the sort of place Maine farmers call "thrifty." Or the farm might be a place of even greater contrast with the surrounding countryside, the spread of a gentleman farmer who lives in a restored eighteenth- or early nineteenth-century country house and keeps horses.

Not all of what many Maine folks would regard as the "real" people of Maine are poor by any means, nor do they all live in mill towns or in the relatively barren countryside. There are also thousands of small businessmen who promote their communities in chambers of commerce and cultivate good fellowship in Kiwanis and Rotary meetings from Kittery and Sanford to Presque Isle and Caribou, and in the larger cities they meet and talk business and politics over lunch in the busy little businessmen's restaurants of Portland and Augusta. At home, they can afford gasoline-powered snowblowers to clear two-car driveways. Their wives do church work and belong to the PTA if they do not hold down a job teaching school or clerking in a shopping plaza, and wives and husbands together go to church suppers and high school basketball games to watch their sons play center and their daughters lead the cheering squad.

Most of the ordinary people of Maine, all the way from the woodcutter living at the official poverty level in a trailer to the car salesman living in a neat ranch house in a postwar housing development, see their state through the eyes of what used to be called "Middle America." For them, Maine's principal needs are for industrial development to make jobs and for energy development, whether in the form of nuclear power plants, offshore drilling, oil refineries, wood-based methanol, or the pursuit of various long-standing dramatic hydroelectric projects, to rescue them from the ever-mounting costs of electricity, home heating, and running cars, tractors, pickup trucks, outboard motors, chain saws, and snowmobiles—all of which are central to the way "Middle Maine" lives. In the sixties and early seventies, they tended to see their economic future and their way of life threatened by outsiders, those who catered to outsiders, and those Maine people who shared the outsiders' expensive, sophisticated tastes and pleasures and their concern for the natural environment. Like Middle Americans generally, the ordinary folk of Maine, at least those away from the coast, tended to feel passed by, neglected by public policy, and resentful of causes and concerns that originated in the comparatively well-off and well-educated middle class.

The emotions generated on both sides by the snowmobile craze illustrate this clash of values as well as anything. Bill Ward, the plumber and bottled gas dealer of Steep Falls, achieved national notice early in 1972 when Berkeley Rice published a piece on snowmobiling in the *New York Times Magazine*. Bill and his neighbors used to spend their winters cooped up in the house watching television, with perhaps a little ice fishing now and then. Now all of Steep Falls, like residents of many such places in Maine, drives around the winter countryside on snowmobiles—"machines," they call them. The attractions of the snow machine are many, Berkeley Rice reports: "With minimal exertion . . . you can go out where only hikers, cross-country skiers and snowshoers went before. You can enjoy a sense of freedom and power that comes rarely to the millions of Americans who spend most of their lives trapped behind desks, in commuter traffic or on assembly lines." [2]

2. Berkeley Rice, "The Snowmobile Is an American Dream Machine," *New York Times Magazine*, February 13, 1972, p. 26.

Snowmobiling has brought the Ward family together, and it has fostered a community spirit in Steep Falls, doing for the social life of the town what church socials and the Grange used to do. The kind of togetherness that goes with belonging to the Saco River Sno-Jockeys or similar clubs and the outdoor exhilaration of it all are a new thing to the many ordinary Maine people who have always gone out after their deer and cut up a store of firewood in the fall, but retreated indoors for most of the winter. A whole culture has built up around the snowmobile, a sort of gasoline alley version of the ski culture that "Middle Maine" has tended to avoid even though there are nearly sixty ski areas in the state.

For another large category of Maine people, however, including all the "newcomers" who live there to get away from the noise and crowds of the city, the snowmobile is a symbol of everything they fear and despise. For one thing, it is terribly noisy. For another, at least in the eyes of those most concerned with ecology, it damages the environment. For their part, snowmobilers accuse the ecologists of being too "finicky" and the new vacation homeowners of trying to prevent them from enjoying land to which they have always had access. Rice understands the importance of the snowmobile as a symbol in a cultural conflict. True, he overlooks the fact that the well-heeled often own snowmobiles and that there are plenty of working-class landowners who resent the intrusion of the machine as much as their sophisticated, prosperous neighbors do. But there is nevertheless a painful truth in his observation:

> This dispute involves much more than the snowmobile, which is merely a symbol in a culture clash between "them" and "us"—between vacation-home owners up from the suburbs and North-country natives who resent the "outsiders" buying up "our" land and keeping "us" from enjoying it; between those who like their pleasures in quiet privacy and those who enjoy noise and crowds. In a survey of snowmobilers in Maine, two-thirds identified themselves as blue-collar workers; three-quarters had never attended college; more than half earned less than $10,000. Vacation-home owners and those concerned about the environment tend to be the educated upper-middle class. . . . The same class

warfare over noise and the environment takes place each summer between those who sail and those who roar past in motor boats.[3]

Useful as the snowmobile is as a symbol, however, this reduction of the clash between the machine and the environment to a species of "class warfare" is a bit too pat. Almost everybody who lives in Maine, of whatever condition or length of residence, is haunted by the ambiguities involved in making decisions about Maine's future. From the post–Civil War industrial "takeoff" period until very recently, the big textile, paper, and shoe manufacturing companies were perceived on all sides as the chief allies and benefactors of Maine's work force and the chief adversaries of the summer people and vacation interests. The predominance of this perception was one reason that big business, especially the paper industry, which owns 52 percent of the land in Maine, has been able over the decades to apply such enormous political clout in the state legislature, which has responded not only to industry's skillful, well-financed lobbies but also to the obvious need for blue-collar jobs for the majority of citizens. It is also the reason that further industrial development got top priority in state programs throughout most of the 1950s and 1960s. By the mid-seventies, neither the division of interests nor the priorities seemed quite so simple.

Consider as evidence the evolving public concerns of Edmund S. Muskie of Rumford, one of Bates College's most illustrious products, who as United States senator, vice-presidential candidate, and contender for the Democratic presidential nomination brought Maine into the national spotlight in his day as Hannibal Hamlin and James G. Blaine did in a similar way in the nineteenth century. When Muskie broke the traditional Republican hold to win the governorship in 1954, he did so with a promise of finding new jobs through industrial development. He soon moved on to the Senate, where in the 1960s he became one of the nation's earliest and most articulate spokesmen for protecting the natural environment and a leading sponsor of legislation aimed at curbing air and water pollution. Then in 1975,

3. Rice, "The Snowmobile," p. 33.

responding to the Middle East oil embargo and the overwhelming American consciousness of dwindling reserves of fossil fuel, Muskie addressed the Senate in favor of further research and development in nuclear energy—thereby rebuking the most adamant of the environmentalists—while insisting that commercial nuclear development go slowly and cautiously enough to allow its interruption whenever potential environmental dangers should so dictate.

This struggle by one especially prominent Maine public figure to solve the delicate calculus of jobs, energy, and the environment probably reflects the fundamental outlook of most of the thoughtful people of Maine—leaving aside the expected partisan wrangling over emphasis and details, and omitting zealots on all sides. One could, for example, fit two more recently arrived Maine public figures into pretty much the same scheme. Kenneth M. Curtis, nominated Democratic national chairman by President-elect Jimmy Carter at the end of 1976, served as governor of Maine in the late 1960s and early 1970s, just at the time that Senator Muskie was most heavily concerned with environmental issues. Early in 1970, he was a leader in a bipartisan drive for innovative legislation designed to protect Maine lands and waters from the dangers of unregulated industry. Two years later, while by no means having abandoned his environmental concerns, Governor Curtis was expressing his parallel concern for jobs and economic development by supporting, against some opposition, the creation of a Maine Industrial Port Authority that would offer tax incentives to encourage the development of industry, including oil refineries on the coast. The governor, however, proposed that any refineries and satellite petroleum industries be made subject to the "full range of Environmental Improvement Commission regulations." [4] Then in 1975, James B. Longley, a fifty-year-old insurance man who had grown up and worked in the textile mills of Lewiston before going to Bowdoin, was elected on his first attempt at public office as an independent candidate for governor. His main appeal, which happened also to be in the spirit of the times nationally as

4. *New York Times,* March 5, 1972, Section 3, p. 17.

the result of the recent Watergate scandals in Washington, was that he was not a "politician"—and that he intended to purge and purify the political process in Augusta, and to cut state spending. But he also combined a concern for jobs and the environment by pledging to attract high-paying, nonpolluting industries to the state. These evolving concerns, reflected in the main emphases of these public figures, indicate the way the questions have been shifting lately.

Take Machiasport. The bay where sailors with pitchforks seized the *Margaretta* in 1775 has now for many years, because of its deep protected waters, its relative proximity to Europe, and its potential for serving an economically depressed area, been considered a prime candidate for development as a deep-water port, oil depot, and refinery site. For a time in the late sixties and early seventies, Machiasport was the latest in a string of projects, beginning with the sixty-year-old dream of harnessing the great tides of Passamaquoddy Bay, for bringing new economic vitality to the far eastern corner of Maine. Support of the Machiasport project was at its most enthusiastic about 1968, when the state government was thinking primarily of heavy industry in its quest for economic development. Then came some serious oil spills in the Atlantic, conflict between the federal and state governments over offshore drilling rights on the continental shelf (later resolved by the Supreme Court in favor of the federal government), the failure of an anticipated change in oil import quotas that would have been to the advantage of the project, and a dramatically rising concern over possible damage to the natural beauty of the Maine coast. The idea became surrounded by reservations even by some of its most avid former backers until by the middle of the seventies, Machiasport simply was not being discussed any more. There was, however, talk of other oil refineries, especially one costing $500 million at desperately impoverished Eastport, where one of its 2,000 residents told a writer for *Down East* magazine in 1976, "If you could exchange food stamps for bus tickets, we'd all be gone." [5] At the end of 1976, the federal Environmental Protection Agency

5. Art Grinell, "Quoddy Power," *Down East* 22 (June 1976): 72.

was still pondering that proposal, which was being backed as usual by those concerned with economic development in Maine and New England and opposed as usual by most environmentalists and the fishing interests, joined this time by some Canadian interests concerned about the dangers of heavy traffic in the narrow channel between Maine and New Brunswick.

One effect of the proposed Eastport refinery, at least as its plans stood in 1976, would be to end a half-century of discussion about generating power from the tides of Passamaquoddy. The refinery and the tidal power project appear to be incompatible because both projects propose to use some of the same openings between islands, one for tidal dams and one for tanker channels.

The Passamaquoddy scheme rivals the nineteenth-century dream of an international railroad and steamship link for audacity and ingenuity, and its father, Dexter P. Cooper, rivals John Alfred Poor as a practical visionary whose plans for Maine seem, like Poor's, doomed to defeat by inertia and politics. Cooper, a hydroelectric engineer trained in Germany and experienced with some of the world's biggest waterpower projects, came up with the idea in 1919. If a series of dams and locks were built across the mouths of Passamaquoddy and Cobscook bays, 70 billion cubic feet of tidewater—more water than flows down the Mississippi River in two weeks—could be admitted twice each day to Passamaquoddy, the upper bay, while the flood tide could be kept out of Cobscook, the lower bay, altogether. Then, just at the crest, the locks that had admitted the flood tide to Passamaquoddy could be closed and the trapped water allowed to surge over a twenty- to thirty-foot drop through generating turbines into Cobscook Bay, whose locks would then be opened to allow the water to return again to the sea. An auxiliary station fifteen miles away, operating from a reservoir filled by pumps during the ebb, would generate power during the hours that Passamaquoddy was filling again.

Cooper was more than an engineer. Like Poor before him, he saw his project as the centerpiece in a chain of interdependent developments that would transform an already decaying Eastport region into a thriving industrial center. And he began the work himself—test borings, surveying, an elaborate working scale model, selling the plan to Westinghouse, Boston Edison, General Electric, and Middle West Industries, getting preliminary permits from authorities in the United States and Canada, and putting in $85,000 of his own money. Then came the stock market crash of 1929. The bankers moved out, and Cooper went to the Soviet Union to take charge of the hydroelectric development at Dnepropetrovsk.

The plan came alive again with the New Deal. Franklin D. Roosevelt, after all, was a summer resident of the area and a friend of Cooper's. Roosevelt thought of "Quoddy" as one of the relief projects of his first administration, to be headed this time by the Army Corps of Engineers. And it almost went. But it was beaten on the state level by a powerful coalition of Maine's big three power companies—Central Maine Power, Bangor Hydro-Electric, and Cumberland County Light—which successfully opposed the creation of a Quoddy Authority by the state legislature out of fear that the federally funded project would force down electricity rates, and in Congress by the two Maine senators who refused to play ball with the South by backing the Florida Ship Canal in return for southern support for Quoddy.

Now only some abandoned, unfinished riprap dams and a sad, ramshackle village of forty-year-old government workers' houses remind the people of Washington County of the abortive start the engineers made on the project in 1936. If the timing of the start of construction was political, Roosevelt and the engineers might just as well have saved their time, since Maine was one of the two states to go against the New Deal that presidential election year anyway. Dexter Cooper died in 1938, defeated and broke. Like John Poor, who had died amidst the shambles of a magnificent dream in 1871, Cooper had tested a brilliant vision against Maine granite and the greed of private interest. And lost.

The question, of course, is whether Cooper's dream is really dead. The high cost of oil in the 1970s, the obvious need for some kind of economic boost to what may well be the most impoverished part of a generally poor state, and the relative cleanliness of hydroelectric power all combine to suggest that the scheme may still be worth looking into. It is technologically feasible and has been for more than half a century; but questions remain about its cost-effectiveness compared to oil-fired steam generators and to nuclear power plants like the one that Maine Yankee started at Wiscasset in 1972. There are also environmental questions even with a project like this because of the effects on temperature and salinity that will come from impounding tidewater. There is the Eastport refinery project, and also the possibility that the Canadian government may get there first with tidal power by damming off the head of the Bay of Fundy, where the tides are even more gigantic than at Quoddy, with money from the Rothschilds of London. If that should happen, there probably would be little need for Quoddy because New England would be buying cheap Canadian power then. No one of these problems, however, is the sort of thing that beat John Poor and Dexter Cooper.

The idea of building publicly financed hydroelectric plants high on the Saint John River has been around almost as long as the idea of the Quoddy project. Recent discussion, in fact, frequently ties the two projects together. Here again, the power companies—apparently favoring the nuclear route for future development—have responded with the rhetoric of private enterprise, supported both by the big paper companies whose woodlands would be affected and by some environmentalists who are concerned about the effects of flooding portions of the wilderness.

Machiasport, refineries, atomic power plants, Passamaquoddy, the Dickey-Lincoln School power project on the Saint John: like the snowmobile, these are symbols of competing, often clashing values and concerns about the future of Maine —values and concerns that can mingle and tug ambiguously, confusingly, and passionately in the same concerned mind. Unlike the snowmobile, however, these are more than symbols. They are also issues. And they are the kind of issues whose wise resolution is crucial to the future welfare of Maine as a place and the people who live there. Unfortunately, Maine's past record in dealing with issues of this nature does not provide grounds for as much confidence in their wise resolution as one might wish.

There has been in the recent past, however, the growing recognition that these and questions like them are not several issues but one. The issue is as large and complicated as any state has ever had to face, and so to expect consensus after a few years of dispassionate study and good-humored debate is to expect the impossible. The process of its resolution will be neither simple nor pleasant. But it is a single issue nevertheless: working out a policy of development and conservation for the next several decades that in its simplest terms comes down to balancing the equation of jobs, energy, and the environment. This is hardly an issue unique to Maine, but the setting is unique, and as usual Maine has some special problems and opportunities. The state has, in fact, taken some unusual steps already toward recognizing the inseparability of the various proposals for economic development and natural conservation.

Sometime in the 1960s, the gradually emerging consciousness of the earth's smallness, of its ultimate finiteness as a provider of resources and supporter of life, merged with the equally powerful stream of discontent with industrial pollution, urban ugliness, and suburban boredom—the mounting concern for "the quality of life." These two powerful streams, one ecological and the other psychosocial, combined to arouse a new awareness, from without the state and from within it, of the value of unspoiled land in Maine, especially on and near the coast. Maine had not really had a land boom since the exciting antebellum years in Bangor, but there was one on now. Shore property soared in price, and the almost frantic quest for a piece of the Maine shoreline had by the seventies pushed all the way down east to Lubec. Here was a new factor in the question; this was not simply the need to consider the tourist industry and the summer residents, but the realization that in the last quarter of the twentieth century, the intrinsic value of undeveloped Maine land might well have to take precedence over some development schemes simply as a hard-nosed, economic fact of life. And as land values soared, so did taxes—which made it harder for long-term and hereditary owners to resist the pressures to sell out.

Against that background and the mounting concern about oil pollution, the Maine legislature moved to protect the state's increasingly valuable shoreline from potential damage. Early in 1970, a ground-breaking law gave the state Environmental Resources Commission licensing power over all major industrial commercial development. A companion law empowered the commission to tax petroleum products in transit through Maine waters so that a fund could be created for cleaning up any oil spills. Both bills got bipartisan support; the principal guidance came from Governor Curtis, a Democrat, and from Harris L. Richardson, the Republican majority leader in the house. A year and a half later, the commission used its new licensing power to deny a permit for an oil refinery on Sears Island in Penobscot Bay. In 1974, the voters approved by more than two to one a $4 million bond issue so the state government could buy up coastal wetlands and upland wildlife habitats to protect them from commercial and residential encroachment. And later the same year, the state and the Great Northern Paper Company agreed to exchange about 59,000 acres of wilderness lands in order to create a continuous parcel of public land embracing both Baxter State Park and the Allagash Wilderness Waterway. Other voices, apparently, were beginning to counteract the traditional, overwhelming, legislative influence of the utilities and the big paper and lumber companies.

Even more encouraging, many of the groups concerned about the environment have done more positive things than simply oppose refineries. Thus the "Allagash Group," the Coastal Resources Action Committee, and the National Resources Council of Maine, among others, have been studying the state's special assets with a view not only to preserving them but also to determining how they can most appropriately contribute to the state's economy—using new ideas, such as "aquaculture," or fish farming. An overall development policy and land use plan, many think, is an essential step if individual decisions are to be made consistently and rationally and if the various competing concerns in the state are to get balanced consideration in the long run.

Jobs, energy, the environment—one big complicated question, complicated still further by the pressures of the coastal land boom. Here is where most of the brains and planning money was going in the 1970s, and it was the arena in which most of the fighting and compromising was being carried out, the arena that commanded the overwhelming attention of all who cared anything about Maine.

But planning and politics do not tell the whole story. The merging streams of consciousness that brought about the coastal land boom have also stimulated a re-examination of life at its most basic levels. One result has been a reaffirmation and even celebration of the values that are a part of the Maine mythology: independence, frugality, harmony with nature, and so on. In thousands of Maine families, the public quest for a state land use plan, clean and economical energy, and nonpolluting industries has its private counterpart in the rediscovery of the wood stove, organic gardening, and even the windmill and the owner-built "energy-efficient" house. Small businesses make wind-powered home electric generators and the "clivus multrum," a composting device that is supposed to be a better way than the flush toilet. "Homesteading" has been reintroduced into the vocabulary, meaning in this time and place the acquiring of a long-abandoned Maine farm and squeezing something close to subsistence out of land that the inflated new prices have not yet reached.

There are points at which this new quest for a fundamental quality in life—what John Cole, the ecologically minded editor of the provocative and controversial *Maine Times* calls "post-industrialism"—touches on the zanily countercultural. Most of the "homesteaders," for example, have never before waded through a barnyard in March, tugged a teat, or slopped a pig, let alone killed one. They are recent refugees, even expatriates, from what they perceive as the mainstream society in other parts of the country. Part of the attraction for this set was Scott Nearing, the ageless guru of organic gardening who had been urging people to get away from the drugstore and back to the land for several decades. At Harborside on Penobscot Bay, he and his wife Helen ran, in 1976, what was probably the world's most famous organic garden, where disciples came for instruction and inspiration.

As romantics—one cannot help but wonder how soon most of the "homesteads" will go the way of Brook Farm—and as intellectuals, the new seekers after self-sufficiency and the traditional Maine idea are, of course, light years removed from the gasoline-powered culture of "middle Maine." Yet the two cultures are neighbors, and in many curious ways, they overlap. As of 1976, Maine was still big enough that its well-known tolerance for eccentricity showed no signs of stretching. Perhaps that, in the end, is what will save the clash of images from being destructive.

11

A Sense of Place

IMAGES. From the Abnakis' Dawnland to the romantics' refuge from civilization and all the perceptions in between, they have been responses to a place. The images of Maine have been shifting and transitory, but no more so than the men and women who have themselves played out the little scenes of human history on a stage that is bigger, more beautiful, and more permanent than history itself. In alternating foaming interpenetration, the surging sea and the implacable granite ledges of the coast were acting out together their rhythmic sacrament of eternity for ages before any Red Paints, Abnakis, Frenchmen, or Englishmen were on hand to reflect upon it, and undoubtedly will continue to do so for ages after the man-made name of Maine has vanished. And the pines and spruces, and the mackerel and herring, and clams and lobsters and shrimp were there, too. Man is completely able and possibly foolish enough to deprive himself of most of these resources over the short run of human history. But in the long run nature is both persistent and forgiving, so it seems more than likely that for a long time after civilization, there will be forms of life like these interacting with the sea and the rocks and the soil and with one another. The gulls, no doubt, will continue to soar and plunge and drop shellfish on the ledges and hold screaming commerce together. And Katahdin, by that or another or no name at all, will brood like the Abnaki god who lived there, dividing lakes

180

and river valleys on the south and west from the high flatlands of Aroostook on the north and east.

But this is a history, and histories are not mainly about the stage but about the actors. And the province of the historian is neither geological time nor eternity, of which the relative permanence of geological time reminds him, but the moment in time during which people have lived in human societies. The human moment in Maine has gone on for some few centuries now; how much longer it will last is for science or theology to figure out, if anyone cares to know, not history. For practical and accepting people like those of Maine, however, the question is not how long it will last but how well. And in the area of quality, history may have discovered some useful lessons.

As this little essay on the Maine past is being brought to a close on the last day of the bicentennial year, a lawsuit by the Penobscot and Passamaquoddy Indians claiming twelve million acres of Maine land worth $25 billion has blocked the issuance of municipal bonds and thrown the state government into shock. And down on Nantucket Shoals, the wreckage of the *Argo Merchant* flounders in two pieces while her cargo, a gelatinous pancake of industrial fuel oil 140 miles long, drifts near the fishing grounds of Georges Bank. The nation watches helplessly this New Year's Eve to see whether the awful potential of the biggest oil spill in American history will be realized. Both of these incomplete episodes are as disturbing for their implications as for their immediate dangers. For both suggest the closeness of human audacity, which is necessary for achievement, to arrogance, which can be destructive and self-defeating.

Technically, the land suit rests on the contention that massive sales of Indian territory in Maine to local and state authorities were invalid because an act of the First Congress restricted land deals with the Indians to the new federal government unless permission were given otherwise. More deeply, the suit has to do with white indifference to modern Indian poverty. It is a manifestation of the contemporary self-assertiveness of various neglected minority groups in American life—once again, the Maine version of a national phenomenon is singular and unexpected—and a symptom of the recent recognition of the value of

Maine land. On the deepest level of all, however, the suit and all that prompted it remind us of man's preposterous claim to possess nature. This is not to suggest that modern civilization, in view of the point to which history has led us, can do without land titles, as the ancestors of today's claimants did very nicely before the Europeans came. It is only that in his compulsion to own and to dominate that which is bigger and more permanent than he, and even to fight others for ownership and dominion, man can easily forget his transience and his puniness before nature.

The *Argo Merchant* episode, the apparent result of the subordination of care for safety to the drive for profit, betrays similar attitudes. The extraction of the decayed remains of ages-old primitive organisms from the earth in the form of oil in this part of the human moment, and the transformation of oil into the world's one great universal commodity, testify to man's ingenuity, enterprise, and audacity. But with that, we are increasingly aware, has come a certain callousness about nature. Here, too, there is revealed the urge to subdue and to dominate.

But subjection, mankind is just beginning to realize, is not the only possible goal we can entertain toward nature, despite what James Sullivan wrote in his history of Maine at the end of the eighteenth century. On the contrary, it is beginning to appear, nature makes a far better partner than slave.

This book has shown, I hope, how Maine has affected the mind. So far, the natural resources and natural beauty of the place, its placement on the map, and the human attitudes and characteristics that have formed as natural local responses to these particularities have all been strong enough to resist to some degree the tendencies that make for absorption into a larger, uniformly dreary culture. That is part of the reason—no, all of the reason—that Maine remains recognizable for itself rather than as some indistinguishable molecule in a homogenized whole. There are some who will regard this ability to resist as insular, backward, and provincial. Indeed, one is forced to admit that the relative weakness of the assault has almost as much to do with the situation as the strength of the resistance, and the assault is weaker here than in some other places for the very reasons of geography and inertia that prevent Maine from participating as fully as most states in the economic life of the nation. Very well, I admit the anomaly, for Maine needs jobs and money and economic vitality, and I even admit to occasional embarrassment over certain aspects of Maine provincialism. Nevertheless, I do not deplore Maine's particularity. I celebrate it. And the reason I celebrate it is the effect of the place on the mind.

To be aware of a resisting yet forgiving nature, to allow special landforms and special climates and, yes, special people and their special artifacts that are as much a part of the landscape as the gulls and the cormorants, to work upon the mind as Maine has worked on the minds of all the generations since the Dawnlanders—all this is to know what it means to regard nature as a partner, not a slave. And it is to acquire a sense of belonging to the place, which is a different thing than having a sense that the place belongs to you.

The partnership between mankind and the particularities of Maine has many symbols. All are symbols that may be opposed, for example, to the symbol that is the broken *Argo Merchant* and its oil slick, a kind of modern *Pequod*. One such symbol is the way in which the unprepossessing man-made structures of coastal Maine—the lighthouses, the gray fishing shacks, the boats and buoys, the orderly contrasts of white and green trimness in villages along sparkling rivers and bays—blend with the natural landscape, complementing not dominating, nestling not paving over. Another is the lobsterman. His rounds are determined by weather and tide, not the clock. The lines of his little craft, developed out of generations of practical experience, craftsmanship, and untutored aesthetic sense, are as clean and graceful as a clipper's, suited perfectly to the job and the waters in which she works. Coming alongside one of his buoys, the lobsterman makes a sure-handed sweep with his hook and hoists the buoy aboard. Then in what seems like one fluid motion, he heads his boat upstream or into the current, cuts his engine to just the right amount of power to counteract the flow of water, flips the line over a winch and hauls in the pot, quickly sorts out the keepers from the culls, rebaits, heaves the pot over the side, pays out the line, lets drop the buoy, gives more throttle to the deep-throated competent but unobtrusive engine, and steers for the next buoy. Depending on the depth of the water and the size of the catch, it has all taken perhaps two or three minutes. Two or three minutes during which man, machine, and nature have acted as a unit that is an unspeakable, tireless pleasure to behold again and again for its flow, its grace, its integration. That is how the lives of men and women ought to be: at home and in graceful, useful partnership with their works, with nature, and with their place.

Maine still offers the opportunity to her people to live this way because Maine has not yet been wholly subdued, not yet enslaved and paved over. Its own unique and natural self still determines, by and large, what happens there and what is thought there. It may, in short, still be enjoyed. With the application of wisdom and creativity, it may even be enjoyed profitably as well as humbly, with respect, and with the aching recognition of beauty and a worthwhile past that in still moments yet tug at a man's soul to let him know that this is home.

Appendix

The Name of Maine

Historians have puzzled over the name of Maine for nearly a century and a half. Some of the earlier, more confident historians probably ought to have been more puzzled than they were. We are told by John S. C. Abbott, who cited William D. Williamson, who cited James Sullivan, who cited nobody, that Sir Ferdinando Gorges and his partner John Mason named the province in honor of the English queen, who had inherited the French Province of Maine. There was indeed a Province of Maine in France, once part of the vast feudal domain that Henry II of England won from Eleanor of Aquitaine but long since returned to French hands.

It is possible that Gorges's Province of Maine derived its name from the French one in some way, but Henrietta Maria, the young French queen of Charles I, did not marry him until May 1625, about a month after Charles ascended the throne. And the first use of the name "Province of Maine" for the American territory was in 1622, when Henrietta Maria was not quite thirteen and young Prince Charles was still considering the charms of the Infanta Maria of Spain. Moreover, it does not appear that title to the Province of Maine ever in fact was transferred from the French crown to the princess.

The other common theory, acknowledged by Williamson and picked up by others, has to do with common seventeenth-century usage. Indeed, we learn from Smith's writings, from William Hubbard's *History of New England* (1680), and from certain early land patents, that the shoreline of these island-studded waters was customarily called "the main," spelled alternately *maine, maigne, mayn, mayne,* and even *meign.* This theory does have the virtue of a certain attractive plausibility, which comes under challenge only when one confronts what Charles Thornton Libby has called the "thunderous tones of finality" in Charles's royal patent of 1625 which regranted part of the territory to Gorges on the condition that it "shall forever hereafter bee called and named the Province or County of Mayne and not by any other name or names what-soever." In the first volume of the *Province and Court Records of Maine* (1928), Libby argues with almost irresistible logic that "if Maine was thus named, it stands almost alone (Newfoundland is one) as an opportunity lost for paying *somebody* a compliment. On the other hand, bearing in mind the French influences about the court at that time . . . it is easy to credit the uniform statements of all the early historians that Maine was named after the French province."

Confronted by all this uncertainty, Maine people should solace themselves with the thought that misty beginnings bespeak antiquity and deep roots. What other American state can claim such a charming lack of clarity in its origins? Readers and scholars interested in following the controversy and perhaps solving the puzzle for themselves should consult Sullivan, *History of the District of Maine,* p. 307; Williamson, *History of the State of Maine,* vol. 1, p. 277; Abbott, *History of Maine,* p. 107; Joshua L. Chamberlain, *Maine: Her Place in History,* p. 54*n.;* Albert Matthews, "Origin of the Name of Maine," *Publications of the Colonial Society of Massachusetts,* vol. 12, pp. 366–380; and *Province and Court Records of Maine,* vol. 1, p. 11, note. For facts of publication see "Suggestions for Further Reading."

Suggestions for Further Reading

If I had just finished reading this book instead of writing it, and were a more-or-less casual reader still interested enough in the Maine past to press on with my discoveries, I think I should turn next to Louise Dickinson Rich. Her view of Maine, like this one, is a personal view. Her writing is anecdotal, breezy, and fun. Her books are not in the least scholarly, but they will tell you many things worth knowing about the history of Maine. By the time you are through with one of them—I would not read both the ones I am about to mention because they overlap somewhat—you will be ready, especially if you have also just read this book, to put the more specialized works in context. The first half of her *State O' Maine* (New York: Harper & Row, 1964) provides a quick introduction to the history of Maine from the Ice Age to statehood. For some reason, writers of Maine history have tended to conclude their chronological treatments about the time of statehood, and then go on to a topical organization or a discussion of contemporary matters. Mrs. Rich is not an exception in this regard. Her other general book on Maine, *The Coast of Maine: An Informal History and Guide* (New York: Thomas Y. Crowell Co., 1975), has been updated several times. It is a good glove compartment companion for the visitor and traveler, and its geographical sections, which are its heart, are introduced by a good compact history, some of which repeats parts of *State O' Maine.*

Good, informative introductory reading, more systematic and less personal than Mrs. Rich's books, can also be found in two expanded updates of the 1937 Maine guidebook prepared by the Maine staff of the Federal Writers' Project, *Maine: A Guide "Down East."* The first revision of the guidebook was the one edited by Ray Bearse, *Maine: A Guide to the Vacation State,* 2nd rev. ed. (Boston: Houghton Mifflin Co., 1969), issued as part of the New American Guide Series. The following year, in observance of the Sesquicentennial of Maine statehood, the Maine League of Historical Societies and Museums came

187

out with its own revision of the guide, edited by Dorris Isaacson, who edited the Federal Writers' version in 1937. This one bears the original title, *Maine: A Guide "Down East,"* and was printed for the League by Courier-Gazette of Rockland. These books, like those of Mrs. Rich, are good glove compartment guides for the traveler and offer a most pleasant and useful introduction to Maine places and the Maine past.

With the appetite thus whetted—or, if one is already of more scholarly inclinations, he might skip the appetizer altogether—the reader ought to be ready for more serious history. Unfortunately, there has not been much for many decades by way of good comprehensive state history, even though there has been a most welcome stirring of interest lately in the production of worthwhile monographs on aspects of the Maine past. The best "history of Maine" in history, in my opinion, was William D. Williamson's *History of the State of Maine* (2 vols., Hallowell, Me.: Glazier, Masters & Co., 1832; Freeport, Me.: Cumberland Press, 1966), which quickly superseded in accuracy and thoroughness the first such book on the scene, James Sullivan's *History of the District of Maine* (Boston, 1795; Augusta: Maine State Museum, 1970). I hope it is clear from Chapter Four of the present work why I regard a sensitive reading of Sullivan very much worthwhile, but as a reliable compendium of historical facts, his book does not hold a candle to Williamson's. The fact that Williamson's extraordinarily thorough, scholarly, and judicious history came out only twelve years after statehood amidst a cluster of several carefully researched works by other important amateur Maine historians helps explain why so many writers over the past 145 years have abandoned their story line about 1820. It was Williamson, following and improving upon Sullivan, who fashioned the chronology from his own original research. Unfortunately for those writers who have relied upon him and his generation ever since, Williamson could not write a narrative history of the future any better than the rest of us can.

Despite the leanness of the last century and a half with regard to comprehensive histories of the state, the cupboard is not entirely bare. Of the half-dozen or so attempts since Williamson to write the whole history of Maine, I think Louis Clinton Hatch's *Maine: A History* (1919; Somersworth, N.H.: New Hampshire Publishing Co., 1974) has been the most successful. It is strongest on the nineteenth century, where the organization is largely, but not entirely, topical. Several of the chapters are essays by authors other than Hatch himself. Of these, the most interesting is Fannie Hardy Eckstorm's early chapter on the Maine Indians. The reader in search of a serious book covering the entire history of Maine would also do well to check out a well-chosen selection of readings entitled *A History of Maine: A Collection of Readings on the History of Maine, 1600–1970* (Dubuque, Iowa: Kendall/Hunt Publishing Co., 1969), ed. Ronald F. Banks. Professor Banks's compilation, obviously designed for the classroom in order to fill the terrible void in published materials suitable for college-level courses in the history of Maine, chooses appropriate selections from monographs in order to form a chronological treatment through the nineteenth century, and then relies more heavily on recent articles, both popular and scholarly, to discuss crucial issues of the twentieth century. Though it is hardly a coherent history of Maine—obviously, no collection of readings can be that—Professor Banks has tried harder than the compilers of most such readers to provide continuity and comprehensiveness.

The best-covered area of Maine history probably remains the colonial period. Williamson's history, of course, was devoted overwhelmingly to the colonial and revolutionary periods, as was Sullivan's. But even in our own century, much of the best writing on Maine subjects has focused on colonial beginnings. The most distinguished of this work is that of Henry S. Burrage, whose *Beginnings of Colonial Maine* (Portland: Printed for the state by Marks Printing House, 1914) is an exceptionally scholarly treatment of that topic from the exploration stage in the late fifteenth century to the Massachusetts takeover in 1658. Herbert Edgar Holmes's *Makers of Maine: Essays and Tales of Early Maine History* (Lewiston, Me.: Haswell Press, 1912) was the first of the Maine colonial histories to make extensive use of French materials, and is therefore strong on the French and Jesuit side of early Maine history. Unfortunately, this extremely worthwhile endeavor is marred by a lack of specific documentation and by an obvious effort on the part of its author to correct what he saw as an English, "Puritan" bias in some of the earlier histories by an equally dogmatic, opposite bias of his own. For a recent attempt at a regional social history from settlement to the beginning of the revolutionary crisis, one might look at my own work, *The Eastern Frontier: The Settlement of North-*

ern New England, 1610–1763 (New York: Alfred A. Knopf, 1970), which deals with the populating of New Hampshire and Maine west of the Kennebec, and with some of the problems and people associated with that process. Gordon E. Kershaw's recent study, *The Kennebeck Proprietors, 1749–1775* (Somersworth, N.H.: New Hampshire Publishing Co. for Maine Historical Society, 1975), examines in fascinating detail the rise and decline of one of the great land companies that was responsible for the northeastern expansion of settlement in Maine in the eighteenth century.

To this very brief list of books specifically on the colonial period, I would add two more on a special topic that is of crucial importance to an understanding of the economics and politics of northern New England in the eighteenth century. One is Robert G. Albion's *Forests and Sea Power* (Cambridge, Mass.: Harvard University Press, 1926) and the other is Joseph J. Malone's *Pine Trees and Politics* (Seattle: University of Washington Press, 1964). Both deal with the business of cutting Maine and New Hampshire trees for ship timbers and masts and the relationship between that business and British naval strategy, provincial politics, and the economic and social development of the region. As the titles imply, Albion's older and seminal study covers a great deal more ground than Malone's more recent and more narrowly political study. In addition to these, I recommend Byron Fairchild's *Messrs. William Pepperrell: Merchants at Piscataqua* (Ithaca, N.Y.: Cornell University Press for the American Historical Association, 1954) as a scholarly but readable study of a Maine merchant family. It illuminates the workings of colonial commerce and at the same time tells us about politics and war in colonial New England, since one of the William Pepperrells was also the hero of Louisbourg. And for an extremely compact, highly interpretive discussion of the mutual impact of man and forest in colonial New England as a whole, see Charles F. Carroll, *The Timber Economy of Puritan New England* (Providence, R.I.: Brown University Press, 1973).

The one indispensable book for studying Maine statehood is Ronald F. Banks's *Maine Becomes a State: The Movement to Separate Maine from Massachusetts, 1785–1820* (Middletown, Conn.: Wesleyan University Press for Maine Historical Society, 1970), which covers in detail both the internal political developments that led to the decision for the separation of Maine from Massachusetts and the congressional politics of the Missouri Compromise. Banks did the job so well that his book will not soon be superseded. For the boundary controversy and the so-called "Aroostook War" that followed close on the heels of statehood, the place to look is Henry S. Burrage's *Maine in the Northeastern Boundary Controversy* (Portland: Printed for the state, 1919).

Maine's maritime heritage is ably discussed in three works, each with a different focus and scope, but each with its own virtues. From broadest to narrowest, they are Robert G. Albion, William A. Baker, and Benjamin W. Labaree, *New England and the Sea* (Middletown, Conn.: Wesleyan University Press for the Marine Historical Association, 1972); William H. Rowe's *The Maritime History of Maine* (New York: W. W. Norton & Co., 1948), the standard work on the subject which by now could probably stand an updated successor; and William A. Baker's marvelous local study, *A Maritime History of Bath, Maine and the Kennebec Region* (2 vols., Bath: Marine Research Society of Bath, 1973). If one is especially interested in the fishing industry, he might add Raymond McFarland's old but still reliable *History of the New England Fisheries* (New York: Appleton, 1911).

The two best books on the history of lumbering in Maine, with which a reader might well follow Charles Carroll's brief interpretation of this aspect of the colonial period, are Richard G. Wood, *A History of Lumbering in Maine, 1820–1861* (Maine Studies No. 33, Orono, 1935 and 1961); and David C. Smith, *A History of Lumbering in Maine 1861–1960* (Maine Studies No. 93, Orono, 1972). Professor Smith has helped tie the two books together with an introduction to the 1961 reprint of Wood's book. Most readers would find it interesting to follow up with the Ralph Nader study group's attack on the engrossment of Maine woodlands by the paper companies, reported in William C. Osborn's *The Paper Plantation* (New York: Grossman Publishers, 1974), which has an introduction by Mr. Nader.

The reader who is interested in Maine agriculture must turn to the books on that topic by Clarence A. Day, whose works form a conspicuous part of the second series of the University of Maine Studies. They are *A History of Maine Agriculture, 1604–1860*, no. 68 (Orono, 1954), *Farming in Maine, 1860–1940*, no. 78 (Orono, 1963) and *Ezekiel Holmes, Father of Maine Agriculture*, no. 86 (Orono, 1968).

The literature of the contemporary consciousness of the special quality of Maine life and the debate over its future is growing almost daily, largely in the form of articles in newspapers, magazines, and journals. The reader ought to be especially aware of *Down East,* which stresses the picture-book and historical side of Maine—and does it extremely well—but tends to avoid pointed controversy, and *Maine Times*, which by contrast is overtly political, tending to uphold the side of ecology against what it views as various special interests. One book-length discussion of this general topic that deserves special notice is Richard Saltonstall's *Maine Pilgrimage: The Search for an American Way of Life* (Boston: Little, Brown & Co., 1974). The author, a frequent visitor to Maine over many years, tries to visualize a future for the state that combines economic vitality with the preservation of its natural beauty and recreational advantages.

Finally, the reader, student, researcher, or teacher with any interest at all in Maine and its history will find an indispensable collection of maps (sixty-nine, to be exact) in the Maine Historical Society's principal published contribution to the bicentennial, *Maine Bicentennial Atlas: An Historical Survey* (Portland: Maine Historical Society, 1976), ed. Gerald E. Morris. Unfortunately for me, it appeared just at the moment that the writing of the present little book came to a close.

Index

193

Forests (*Cont.*)
  Lumber, Natural resources, Shipbuilding
French and Indian wars, 48, 62. *See also* King George's War, King William's War, Queen Anne's War
French in Maine: beginnings, 10, 16–18; raids, 39; separateness, 133, 140, 143–145; numbers, 134, 140, 141; status, 140, 145; mentioned, 50, 59, 83, 135, 180. *See also* French and Indian wars, Canada
Fur trade, 10–11, 19, 36, 41–42
Future, 91, 94–95, 170–179

"Garden of the State of Maine," 145–148
Geography: landscape, 8; advantages of, 96–99; size and climate, 97; location, 106, 145; Canadian links, 145; effects of, 183. *See also* Coastal characteristics, Scenic grandeur
German settlers, 49
Gilbert, Sir Humphrey, 4, 5
Gilbert, John, 17
Gilbert, Raleigh, 17
"Gilded Age," 133, 134, 145, 148, 153
Gorges, Sir Ferdinando, 11–14 *passim,* 25, 31, 44, 185
Graves, Samuel, 63, 65
Great Eastern (steamship), 100, 102
Great Northern Paper Company, 133, 139, 177
Guast, Pierre du, 10–11, 16, 28

Halifax (navy yards), 67
Hamlin, Hannibal, 122, 170
Harbors: sites for early settlements, 19, 28; Falmouth, 64–65; advantages of, 97; Portland as seaport, 102, 103, 105. *See also* Coastal characteristics
Highways, 155
Hill, Mark Langdon, 81
Historical consciousness: state and local histories, 86; historical societies, 86, 161, 165; study courses, 160–161; monuments, digs, etc., 164
"Hollanders," 22–23
Holmes, Ezekiel, 146
Holmes, John, 81, 82
"Homesteading," modern, 178
Hospitals for the insane, 118–119

Howard, Oliver Curtis, 123
Hubbard, Gov. John, 115
Humor: "Jack Downing" type, 75, 84, 87, 89–90, 107–108; less-refined type, 88, 108; examples of, 149–150
Hydroelectric projects, 168

Images, 7–15 *passim,* 37, 38, 53, 166–179 *passim,* 180
Immigration: postrevolutionary, 91; French-Canadian, 133–135, 140–145 *passim;* domestic, 134–135; pre-Civil War causes for, 135; European, 141–142
Imperialism in America, 41–51 *passim*
Income, average, 166
Indians: Abnaki, 4–9; trade with, 7–19 *passim;* to be christianized, 29; traits, 35; used in Anglo-French conflict, 39, 50; compared to southern Indians, 56; helped against British, 67; poverty of, 181; lawsuit by, 181. *See also* Indian tribes
Indian tribes: Piscataqua, 20, 42; Pequawket, 50; Norridgewock, 50; Pequod, 183. *See also* Abnaki Passama-quoddy, Penobscot, Saco
Industry: iron manufacture, 49; early crafts and mills, 92–93; heavy, 100; leading, 112; rapid growth, 135–140; depression, 140; sugar, 147; shoes, 170; needs for future. *See also* Energy development
International Paper Company, 139

Jackson, Andrew, 75, 77, 84, 87, 88
Jefferson, Thomas, 24, 53, 69, 77, 82
Jewett, Sarah Orne, 156–158, 159
Jones, Capt. Ichabod, 63–64
Josselyn, John: visits to Maine, 14, 31; books on Maine, and 17, 20; biographical, 31–32; councillor for province, 31–37; description of Indians, 32–35; view of people of Maine, 35–36; mentioned, 29, 43, 53

Kearsarge (ship), 125
Kennebec: and Massachusetts imperialism, 41–42; lands sold to Boston merchants, 42–43; "Kennebeck Purchase," 48; region, 71, 83; shipbuilding, 91–92
Kent, Edward, 113–114
King, William, 77–78, 82, 83–84
King George's War, 48, 49, 58–60